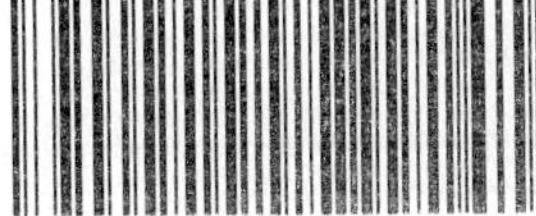

God + The Arts

FINDING REDEMPTION IN THE MOVIES

THE COUNT OF MONTE CRISTO // SECONDHAND LIONS // AN UNFINISHED LIFE // SEABISCUIT

GOD AND THE ARTS

Finding Redemption in the Movies

Published with permission by Serendipity House Publishers, Nashville, Tennessee

ISBN: 978-1-5749-4342-9

Dewey Decimal Classification: 791.43
Subject Headings: MOTION PICTURES—RELIGIOUS ASPECTS/SALVATION

To purchase Serendipity House resources:
ORDER ONLINE www.SerendipityHouse.com
WRITE Serendipity House, 117 10th Avenue North, Nashville, TN 37234
FAX (615) 277-8181
PHONE (800) 525-9563

ALSO IN THE GOD AND THE ARTS SERIES:

Finding Jesus in the Movies ISBN 978-1-5749-4355-9

1-800-525-9563 • www.SerendipityHouse.com

Printed in the United States of America
13 12 11 10 09 08 07 1 2 3 4 5 6 7 8 9 10

CONTENTS

ABOUT GOD AND THE ARTS

Stories, great and small, share the same essential structure because every story we tell borrows its power from a Larger Story. What we sense stirring within is a heart that is made for a place in the Larger Story. What is it about these powerful stories that make us weep, make us laugh, and make our hearts come alive? Is it not that these stories borrow from THE STORY? It is no accident that great movies include a hero, a villain, a betrayal, a battle to fight, a romance, and a beauty to rescue. It is The Epic story. Great movies speak to us because they tell a story, and story is the language of the heart.

Finding Redemption in the Movies is the second release in the **God and the Arts** series, a new small-group Bible study. This experience has been created to guide you on a journey into the one great Epic in which the Bible is set. This fun but challenging study features four films, each with two small-group meetings, *Dinner and a Movie* (Week 1), *Connecting the Dots* (Week 2), and an *Experience Guide* that offers valuable insights. *Dinner and a Movie* night includes conversation starters, ideas for setting the environment, and menu recommendations inspired by the movie. The Bible study experience, *Connecting the Dots*, focuses on connecting significant events and provocative truths from the movie to the Larger Story revealed in the Bible. God has promised to redeem all things (Romans 8:28). Although He is not limited in how He redeems, we know that He redeems through pain, through surrogates, through healing, and through community. As you begin . . .

THE LARGER STORY

He has also set eternity in the hearts of men... (Ecclesiastes 3:11).

Ecclesiastes 3:11 suggests that we come ready-made to understand the greatest story, the epic story, of betrayal and an enemy, of the fight between the destroyer and the redeemer, of something lost and the journey to recovery, of a hero and ultimate restoration. The Larger Story is the story of the gospel and Scripture provides the backstory, the truth, behind every story we tell. In the beginning—during the time before time—there was perfect fellowship among the Triune Godhead and the angelic beings that He created. Act 1 of the Larger Story includes perfection and harmony and it describes beauty, mystery, and order. Act II begins as pride enters the arch-angel Lucifer's heart. Evil enters the story and with it the Villain. Lucifer rebels, he becomes known as Satan, order is tainted, and the villain is expelled from the heavenly realm with his followers. Genesis 1 begins Act III of the Great Story as the dust still settles from this great war. Act III accounts for most of the Bible and human history. It is a story about a daring, redemptive mission that introduces the Hero-Redeemer and climaxes with the cross and resurrection. Act III continues through today and will continue until the ultimate restoration and paradise regained in Act IV.

EXPECTATION

- Experience God through the language of story (Hebrews 1:1).
- Learn to listen to and treasure your heart (Proverbs 4:23).
- As your heart awakens and begins to speak, you may be surprised at what it reveals to you. Our deepest-held beliefs may not be what we think or say we believe (Psalm 51:6).
- Listen for the call of the crucial role you have in the Larger Story (Deuteronomy 20:3).

LANGUAGE OF STORY

Jesus used story as He taught. If He were to come today, He would continue to use story because story is the language of the heart. Through story Jesus is able to communicate on several different levels for sure, but through story He is also able to draw from our own experiences—our own story. This is what you feel when you sense the lump in your throat. Your heart has the ability to recognize in the arts the crucial role you are called to play in the Larger Story. Pay attention to what moves you.

DISCLAIMER

Serendipity House doesn't approve of every word, action, or scene in the movies you'll be engaging. Often the best stories—even in the Bible—include some pretty unsavory characters and behavior. Even a number of the heroes of the Bible displayed some pretty ungodly, unsavory, and questionable behavior. (Abraham, Jacob, Rahab, and David come to mind.) Please note that these movies are not suitable for every situation. It has not been created for a mix of kids and adults or for kids alone. Maturity is a prerequisite.

BEST USE

Finding Redemption in the Movies has several uses:

1. Good fit for normal breaks between book or other Bible studies
2. Perfect fit for special events or retreats
3. A great 8-week small-group study*
4. Content suitable for teaching and preaching illustrations
5. Stand-alone conversations for each of the four movies

MADE FOR MORE

The stirring in your soul is more than "just a moment." It's a reminder that we are made for more than what we are. We have all been created to be His image bearers—chosen from all of creation to play a significant role. Although we have fallen and suffer the consequences, sin is not what's truest about those who have received a new heart in Christ. The Great Stories remind us that we are being called into something grand. Adventure awaits. Listen.

NAVIGATING REDEMPTION IN THE MOVIES

DINNER AND A MOVIE — WEEK 1

SETTING THE STAGE Preparation for the conversation and dinner in addition to ways for enhancing the physical environment. Setting the Stage includes The Buzz, The Story, The Menu, Decor, and Another World.

THE BUZZ The journey you will be taking will be quite a bit different from what most critics might imagine. It's always good to get a feel for how people reacted to the movie at the time. Comments have been found at various places and with little regard to how crazy, uninformed, or misguided they may be.

THE STORY *Finding Redemption in the Movies* will generate a discussion *inspired* by events in the movie, but not necessarily *about* events in the movie. Providing the plot in advance will get the group there quicker.

THE MENU It couldn't be Dinner and a Movie without ... dinner. Serendipity House has created a menu and included recipes at www.SerendipityHouse.com and in the Experience Guide beginning on **page 51**. Recipes have been chosen based on some connection to the movie. Make dinner a group activity—always a great time—or assign dishes to group members.

DÉCOR You, as a group, can make the environment as fun and engaging as you want. Props and ideas for making the environment a part of the experience are included in the Experience Guide beginning on **page 51**. Dinner and a Movie night is about a good time so make it fun.

ANOTHER WORLD The world of film asks us to willingly suspend disbelief in order to move into the world of these experiences. Each group member is asked to leave behind the shadows of reality and step into the world of these respective movies. This brief element of Dinner and a Movie will get you underway.

ON THE LOOK OUT To make Dinner and a Movie even more interesting, we'll give you a clue for finding various miscues, tiny details, or other mistakes. Our goal is to keep everybody's head in the game.

ROLL 'EM It couldn't be Dinner and a Movie without ... the movie. You may choose to watch the movie over dinner or you may choose to have dinner prior to watching the movie. Or you may let the Prologue dictate how you plan this aspect of the *Finding Redemption in the Movies* experience.

PROLOGUE The prologue is for cooking chat, dinner time discussion, or post-movie conversation. This part of the experience can be as light-hearted or deep as you want. These ideas and questions are included to open minds and hearts to the Larger Story elements being revealed.

CONNECTING THE DOTS

WEEK 2

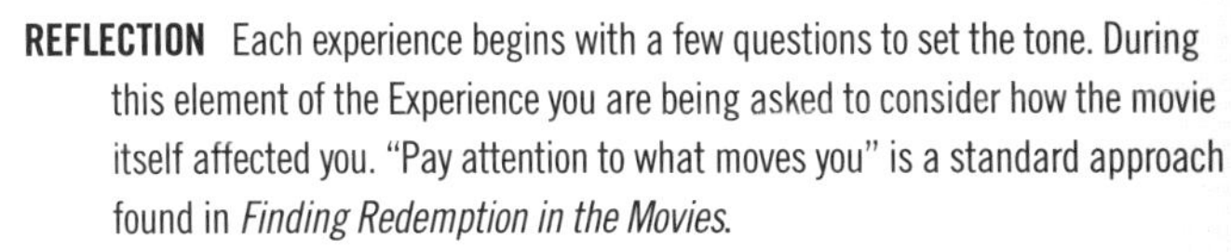

REFLECTION Each experience begins with a few questions to set the tone. During this element of the Experience you are being asked to consider how the movie itself affected you. "Pay attention to what moves you" is a standard approach found in *Finding Redemption in the Movies*.

REWIND Several clips are pulled from each movie to be reviewed during Connecting the Dots. The Rewind icon means "show the clip." Even though we have included time sequences, be aware that these times may vary. We've chosen these clips for several reasons:

- Reinforce an important piece of the Bible study
- Challenge us to look deep into our own stories
- Ask us to consider how art only mirrors a Christian reality
- Point to greater depth
- Support a deeper understanding of the gospel

BACKSTORY Backstory identifies the passages from the Bible that are included in Connecting the Dots. If you were able to strip these characters to their souls you would see a drama unfolding beyond the screen. In the great stories, this is the drama of the heart. This is the story of the Bible.

LIVING LARGE Underway every second in the unseen world of our reality is a larger story—a story unfolding that is more real than the physical world we live and breath in. All who possess a new heart are predisposed to this story. These new hearts recognize the larger story as it is played out on the big screen. This is why you are told, "Pay attention to what moves you."

GOING VERTICAL The experience will always end with a prayer time that includes elements from Connecting the Dots. Going Vertical may include questions to take to God or questions to take to your heart.

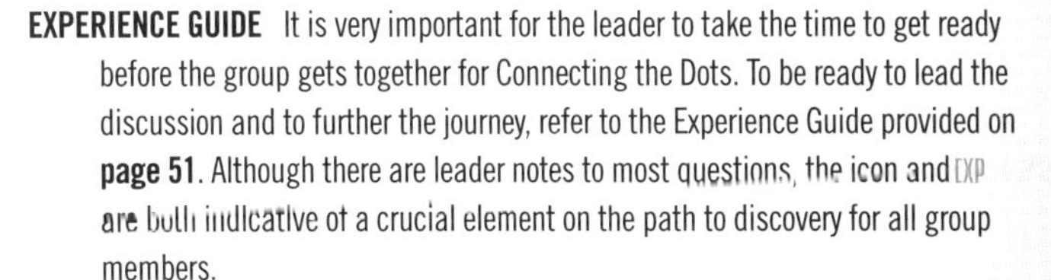

EXPERIENCE GUIDE It is very important for the leader to take the time to get ready before the group gets together for Connecting the Dots. To be ready to lead the discussion and to further the journey, refer to the Experience Guide provided on **page 51**. Although there are leader notes to most questions, the icon and EXP are both indicative of a crucial element on the path to discovery for all group members.

---

*Church-wide usage of movies like the ones used in *Finding Redemption in the Movies* may be subject to restrictions similar to those that apply to music used for congregational singing. To learn more visit www.ccli.com.

NOTES

THE COUNT OF MONTE CRISTO

THE COUNT OF MONTE CRISTO

DINNER AND A MOVIE WEEK 1

The Count of Monte Cristo (2002)
Directed by Kevin Reynolds
Writing credits: Alexandre Dumas, père (novel); Jay Wolpert (screenplay)
Starring: Jim Caviezel, Guy Pearce, Richard Harris
MPAA: Rated PG-13 for adventure violence/swordplay and some sensuality
Runtime: 131 minutes

SETTING THE STAGE

THE BUZZ

"*The Count of Monte Cristo* is the cinematic equivalent of comfort food: familiar and satisfying."
PAM GRADY, REEL.COM

"Hard to resist . . . *The Count of Monte Cristo* is so much fun!"
THE NEW YORK TIMES

THE STORY

Edmond Dantes, an innocent and idealistic young man, is a 19th century sailor. When he makes the naïve mistake of accepting a letter from exiled Napoleon, he stumbles into a larger story of betrayal and intrigue. As a result, Dantes is betrayed by his best friend, Fernand Mondego, who has always been jealous of Dantes' good fortune. Dantes is innocent but sent to prison for treason and tortured there for 13 years. Only a month after his departure to prison, his fiancé weds Mondego after receiving a false report of Dantes' death. When he finally escapes, Dantes' only thoughts are revenge and murder. He is consumed by hate. He receives a map to a fortune found on the island of Monte Cristo and becomes the wealthy Count of Monte Cristo. From there, he travels to France where his former friend and fiancé have relocated as husband and wife. There he fulfills the plans he has dreamed of for years.

THE MENU

And what else would you have for this menu other than Monte Cristo Sandwiches! Ask several members of the group to bring ingredients for the sandwiches, as well as soft drinks, paper goods, and ice. Ask one or two others to prepare the Cassoulet and the Raspberry Trifle ahead of time and bring it to the meeting. Give the guys the sandwich recipe and let them make, cook, and serve the sandwiches along with the

Cassoulet. They will have fun with this. Then ask the women to serve dessert. Use the recipes found in the Experience Guide, or use your own creativity to make your movie and dinner night special. The suggested menu includes:

MONTE CRISTO SANDWICHES
CASSOULET
RASPBERRY TRIFLE

BEFORE STEPPING INTO ANOTHER WORLD ...

- Ask God to speak to you and reveal more of His heart to you in this time.
- Pay attention to what moves you. Be very aware of those moments during which you "feel" something more.
- Take special note of how you feel during specific scenes.
- As you involve yourself in the life of Edmond Dantes, think about your beliefs related to unjust suffering. Does it cause you to question God and His love? Does it make you angry? How could you convince Edmond that God loves him?

ON THE LOOK-OUT

In almost every movie, directors and producers make a few mistakes, and those mistakes are often quite humorous. Look for these goofs in *The Count of Monte Cristo*:

- Overhead power lines and a radio communications tower
- Eye color for a major character
- A blue object along the shoreline

ROLL 'EM

Show *The Count of Monte Cristo.* Following the movie, serve dessert and discuss ideas from the Prologue.

THE PROLOGUE

1. Read the story of Joseph from Genesis 37:1-45:15.
    - How does Joseph's story parallel *The Count of Monte Cristo*?
    - Did Joseph deserve what happened to him?
    - What do you think was going through his mind all those years?
    - Why do you think Joseph just didn't take swift revenge on his brothers? Did he have a right to?
    - At what point during this experience do you think you would have given up hope and faith in God because of this unjust, almost limitless suffering?

TEST YOUR FRENCH TRIVIA

1. How many stages are there in the Tour de France?
   _32 _20 _18 _10

2. What is Dijon?
   _ A famous French wine added to mustard
   _ A famous French soccer player
   _ The site of a famous World War II battle
   _ A city in eastern France

3. What food is Dijon famous for?
   _ Mustard
   _ Hot dogs
   _ Cassoulet
   _ The first McDonalds hamburger in France

4. There are many museums in Dijon, including one dedicated to mustard.
   _True _False

5. Marie Antoinette was the wife of:
   _ Louis VII
   _ Louis XVI
   _ Louis XV
   _ Charles De Gaulle

2. Read the following:

Elie Wiesel was born in 1929 in Transylvania. He was fourteen years old when he and his family were taken from his home to a concentration camp in Auschwitz. His book Night unforgettably records the terrors of his life as an innocent Jewish teenager. Here is a brief excerpt from the book as Elie and his father experience a selection process where some were selected to live and some to die:

"Not far from us, flames were leaping up from a ditch, gigantic flames. They were burning something. A lorry drew up at the pit and delivered its load—little children. Babies! Yes, I saw it–saw it with my own eyes . . . those children in the flames. . . . So this was where we were going. A little farther on was another and larger ditch for adults. I pinched my face. Was I still alive? Was I awake? I could not believe it. How could it be possible for them to burn people, children, and for the world to keep silent? . . .

"Two steps from the pit we were ordered to turn to the left and made to go into a barracks. Never shall I forget that night, the first night in camp, which has turned my life into one long night, seven times cursed and seven times sealed. Never shall I forget that smoke. Never shall I forget the little faces of the children, whose bodies I saw turned into wreaths of smoke beneath a silent blue sky.

"Never shall I forget those flames which consumed my faith forever.

"Never shall I forget that nocturnal silence which deprived me, for all eternity, of the desire to live. Never shall I forget those moments which murdered my God and my soul and turned my dreams to dust. . . . Never."[1]

How does a person keep bitterness from growing in his heart, especially when the situation you are in is absolutely not of your making—and seems hopeless? Have any of you experienced bitterness toward someone who treated you unfairly or turned his back on you, or even just said something very unkind? What was your reaction?

[1]Elie Wiesel, Night (New York: Bantam Books, 1960), pp. 30-32.

3. Think about Joseph from the Old Testament, and Elie Wiesel from more modern times. Is it possible to keep focused on God and forgiveness rather than being held captive by hate and vengeance? Wiesel writes about the "silent blue sky" and "that nocturnal silence." How would you respond to someone who asks you, "How can I believe in God when I am hurting so badly and God is so silent?"

REFLECTION

1. During our last meeting we watched *The Count of Monte Cristo.* Were there any scenes that impacted you—either made you feel passionately emotional or left you with a "lump in your throat"? Explain.

2. What was this movie about? What were the plots and subplots and themes?

3. In *The Count of Monte Cristo* we are introduced to several characters. Who were they and what were their roles?

4. Which of these characters did you identify with the most? Why?

5. Describe the extent and levels of Edmond's suffering.

6. If you were Edmond, which of these would have hurt you the most?

7. Do you think Edmond did anything to contribute to the events that led to his imprisonment and injustice?

CLIP #1: *Characters Revealed*
Chapter 3: ***The New Captain*** *(start @ beginning and end @ 4:42)*

---

1. Very early in the movie we are introduced to Edmond Dantes and Fernand Mondego. What are they like? How are they different? How do you feel about each?

2. Later in the movie Edmond asks Fernand why he turned his back on him and deceived him as a friend. And Fernand answers, "Because you're the son of a clerk, and I'm not supposed to want to be you." What does this quote reveal about Fernand's motivation?

3. It is generally held that Isaiah 14:12-15 and Ezekiel 28:12-17 provide the back-story to the Villain and existence of evil in our world. How does Fernand Mondego's character parallel the Villain in the larger story?

> Your heart became proud because of your beauty; For the sake of your splendor you corrupted your wisdom. So I threw you down to the earth; I made a spectacle of you before kings.
> **EZEKIEL 28:17**

CLIP #2: *A Larger Story*
Chapter 25: ***Villefort*** *(start @ :55 and end @ 4:30)*

---

4. What were the real reasons for Edmond's suffering and imprisonment? What was going on in France and in Villefort's family? Talk about this subplot.

> [6]One day the sons of God[a] came to present themselves before the LORD, and Satan also came with them. [7]The LORD asked Satan, "Where have you come from?" "From roaming through the earth," Satan answered Him**, "and walking around on it." [8]Then** the LORD said to Satan, "Have you considered My servant Job? No one else on earth is like him, a man of perfect integrity, who fears God and turns away from evil." [9]Satan

MONDEGO (to Mercedes): Make love to me.

MERCEDES: Will you ever give up?

MONDEGO: He doesn't have to know.

MERCEDES: I'd know.

MONDEGO: So would I. It'd be our little secret.

MERCEDES: I don't believe in secrets.

MONDEGO: You think Edmond doesn't have secrets? He does. Ask him.

MERCEDES: I know what you want, Fernand.

MONDEGO: You do!

MERCEDES: Remember when we were kids and Edmond got that whistle for his birthday, and you got a pony? You were so mad Edmond was happier with his whistle than you were with your pony. And I'm not going to be your next whistle. . . .

EDMOND (meeting his friends): Hey! . . .

MONDEGO: Yours is a life truly blessed, Edmond.

EDMOND: You're still the best man.

MONDEGO: I know.

COUNT: I was just curious. Why did you tell Countess Mondego 16 years ago that Edmond Dantes had been executed?

VILLEFORT: I don't understand. What on earth are you talking about?

COUNT: It's a perfectly simple question.

VILLEFORT: How do you know these things? You don't understand. Dantes was accepting a letter from Napoleon. That was clearly treason.

COUNT: But we both know he never delivered it. Packing a man off to prison with such knowledge is bad enough. But to tell . . .

VILLEFORT: Your grace, I have no idea what is provoking this perverse discussion.

COUNT: Now I ask myself, "What did my old friend Villefort stand to gain by telling Mercedes that Edmond Dantes is dead?"

EDMOND DANTES: I don't believe in God.

ABBE FARIA: It doesn't matter. He believes in you.

answered the LORD, "Does Job fear God for nothing? [10]Haven't You placed a hedge around him, his household, and everything he owns? You have blessed the work of his hands, and his possessions are spread out in the land. [11]But stretch out Your hand and strike everything he owns, and he will surely curse You to Your face."[12]"Very well," the LORD told Satan, "everything he owns is in your power. However, you must not lay a hand on Job himselfl." So Satan went out from the LORD's presence.

JOB 1:6-12

5. Read Job 1:6-12 above. How do these unseen factors that affected Edmond so significantly parallel the unseen elements in Job's life?

6. Was Job at fault for his suffering? Given the back-story seen in Job 1:6-11, talk about circumstances (good or bad) as a legitimate indicator of God's favor or disfavor. (EXP-58)

7. As a result of the injustice and pain he experienced, Edmond denounced God. How did you feel about his reaction to God's "love"? Do you think he was justified in his belief? How did the priest respond?

[13]As a father has compassion on his children, so the LORD has compassion on those **who fear Him. [14]For He knows what** we are made of, remembering that we are dust.

PSALM 103:13-14

8. Read Psalm 103:13-14 above. How do you think God feels when our faith becomes messy and falters like Job's?

CLIP #3: *He Sees Everything*
Chapter 7: ***Chateau d'If*** *(start @ 2:15 and end @ 3:30)*

9. What was written on the wall of his cell when Edmond arrived at Chateau d'If?

10. How do the words of Dorleac here mimic the Villain in our story?

And we know that God causes all things to work together for good to those who love God, to those who are called according to His purpose.
ROMANS 8:28 (NAS)

Can the One who shaped the ear not hear,
the One who formed the eye not see?
PSALM 94:9

No creature is hidden from Him, but all things are naked and exposed to the eyes of Him to whom we must give an account.
HEBREWS 4:13

Friends, do not avenge yourselves; instead, leave room for His wrath. For it is written: **Vengeance belongs to Me; I will repay**, says the Lord.
ROMANS 12:19

11. Read Romans 8:28 above. Notice that the verse above doesn't say that God causes all things. What does it say? And how does this correspond with what God says in Psalm 94:9, Hebrews 4:13, and Romans 12:19? (EXP-59)

EDMOND: God has no place here priest.
ABBE FARIA: What has replaced him?
EDMOND: Revenge.

See to it that no one falls short of the grace of God and that no root of bitterness springs up, causing trouble and by it, defiling many.
HEBREWS 12:15

DORLEAC: And if you're thinking just now, "Why me, O God?" the answer is God has nothing to do with it. In fact, God is never in France this time of year.

EDMOND: God has everything to do with it. He's everywhere. He sees everything.

DORLEAC: All right, let's make a bargain, shall we? You ask God for help, and I'll stop the moment he shows up (begins to whip Edmond).

JACOPO: I understand you are mad.

EDMOND: Mad? My enemies are falling into my traps perfectly!

JACOPO: Mad, your grace, for not seeing this: you have a fortune, a beautiful woman who loves you. Take the gold, take the woman, and live your life! Stop this plan, take what you have won!

EDMOND: I can't.

JACOPO: Why not?

EDMOND: If you ever loved me, don't rob me of my hate. It's all I have.

MERCEDES: I don't know what dark plan lies within you. Nor do I know by what design we were asked to live without each other these 16 years. But God has offered us a new beginning.

EDMOND: God?

MERCEDES: Don't slap His hand away.

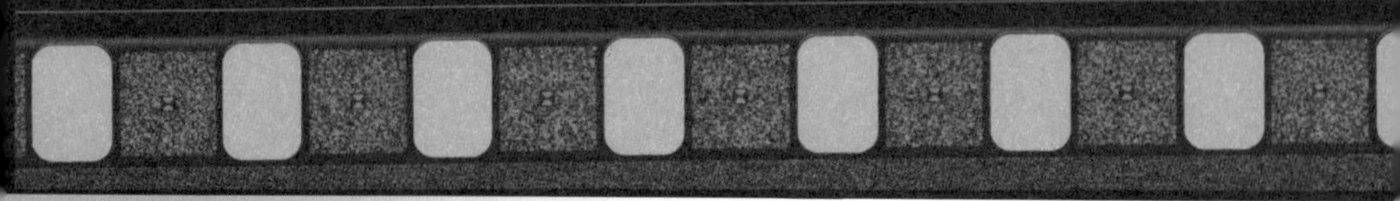

12. From the quotes in the sidebar on page 17, it is evident that Edmond exchanged one prison cell for another. What was that? According to Hebrews 12:15, why would God tell us that vengeance is His territory and for us to "keep out"?

13. When Edmond got to taste the fruit of vengeance, did it heal his wounds and satisfy his soul? Explain.

ABBE: Do not waste the light.

EDMOND: You were a soldier, priest. So you know weaponry. Teach me. Or dig alone.

ABBE: You force me to walk a fine line, Dantes . . . The stronger swordsman does not necessarily win. It is speed! Speed of hand. Speed of mind.

CLIP #4: *Edmond the Student*
Chapter 11: ***Neglect Becomes Our Ally*** *(start @ 2:55 and end @ 12, 2:20)*

---

14. Was there grace in the midst of injustice? Did anything good come from Edmond's two captivities? If so, what?

15. What does Romans 8:35-39 tell us about suffering? (EXP-61)

Who can separate us from the love of Christ? Can affliction or anguish or persecution or famine or nakedness or danger or sword? As it is written: Because of You we are being put to death all day long; we are counted as sheep to be slaughtered. No, in **all these things we are more than** victorious through Him who loved us. For I am persuaded that neither death nor life, nor angels nor rulers, nor things present, nor things to come, nor powers, nor height, nor depth, nor any other created thing will have the power to separate us from the love of God that is in Christ Jesus our Lord!

ROMANS 8:35-39

CLIP #5: *God Is in Everything*
Chapter 26: ***Mercedes and Edmond*** *(start @ beginning and end @ 2:30)*

MERCEDES: Why did you not come to me?

EDMOND: Why did you not wait? You married the very man who betrayed--

MERCEDES (shows Edmond the chord around her finger): I told you that night on the rocks, remember? That it would never leave my finger. And it never has.

EDMOND: Why?

MERCEDES: You know why.

16. What truth about God finally breaks through Edmond's pain and bitterness and sets him free? How can this truth be so powerful and deliver redemption to us?

17. What have you learned about God from this movie? (EXP-62)

GOING VERTICAL

Suffering is something very real in all of our lives. We all will experience it at some point.

During this prayer time, think through the suffering that is going on.

- Be honest (Psalm 103:14)
- Trust God and each other in being able to handle raw honesty
- Thank Him in that He does not require us to take on the role of avenger. Prayerfully leave this responsibility to Him.
- Thank God that He doesn't waste our pain; that Him for redeeming what was meant to cause great harm by the enemy.

Pray that the Holy Spirit will give you the words and means to make a difference in someone else's life who is experiencing pain.

NOTES

SECONDHAND LIONS

SECONDHAND LIONS

DINNER AND A MOVIE WEEK 1

Secondhand Lions (2003)
Directed by Tim McCanlies
Writing credits: Tim McCanlies
Starring: Michael Caine, Robert Duvall, and Haley Joel Osment
MPAA: Rated PG for thematic material, language, and action violence
Runtime: 109 min

SETTING THE STAGE

THE BUZZ

"Written and directed with great care and creativity by Tim McCanlies, *Secondhand Lions* oozes with rural Texas atmosphere circa the 1960s. The more I think about it, the more certain I am that *Secondhand Lions* will end up on my best-of-year list for 2003."

BETTY JO TUCKER, REELTALK MOVIE REVIEWS

"It's been a while since I was sorry that a film was over, but that's how I felt when the final credits for *Secondhand Lions* rolled."

ROB THOMAS, THE CAPITAL TIMES

THE STORY

In this wonderful story, two eccentric recluses (with the help of an aging lion) help transform their abandoned 14-year-old nephew from a boy who doesn't smile into a boy with reason to celebrate. In return, the changed teenager gives both men something to live for. All three find redemption, healing, and love.

Walter is a simple teenage boy who knows nothing about farm life when his mother forces him to live with his great-uncles (Garth and Hub) on their rural Texas farm. But none of them is happy about it. And Walter's mother isn't exactly motivated by family love. Rumors abound that the eccentric recluses (who disappeared under mysterious circumstances for 40 years) are sitting on millions of dollars. She hopes a little bonding time with Walter will result in finding the millions and taking them for herself and her new boyfriend. Eventually Garth warms to Walter and starts telling him stories about those missing 40 years. Hub was a swashbuckling adventurer who led armies in the French Foreign Legion and battled an evil sheik for the love of a beautiful Arabian princess—Jasmine. As the relationship between the three becomes a strong bond, Walter has to make a choice. As he and his mom leave the farm for the last time, Walter tells his mom he wants to go back.

For the first time in his life, he has found security, happiness, and love through the lives of his two old uncles. And Garth and Hub—never too old to learn—discover a lesson on life and happiness through the eyes of a teenager.

THE MENU

Tonight's menu has a very warm, country feel. In fact, if the weather permits, you might want to have the meal outdoors, then come inside for the movie and dessert afterwards. Because the spare ribs could be expensive to make, you may want to ask participants to bring a dollar or two to help defray the cost. Ask other participants to make the baked beans, potato salad, and dessert. Others could be asked to bring paper products, bread, soft drinks, and ice. Use the recipes found in the Experience Guide, or use your own creativity to make your movie and dinner night special. The suggested menu includes:

BARBECUE SPARE RIBS
TEXAS BAKED BEANS
ZESTY POTATO SALAD
CHOCOLATE ALMOND MOUSSE

BEFORE STEPPING INTO ANOTHER WORLD . . .

- Ask God to speak to you and reveal more of his heart to you in this time.
- Pay attention to what moves you. Be very aware of those moments during which you "feel" something more.
- Take special note of how you feel during specific scenes.
- As you become involved in the lives of these three major characters, think about the connections in your own life. Is there someone in your family with whom you need to connect to help him or her discover redemption? Perhaps there is an older person in your family who needs to know that he or she is loved. Or is there a teenager who, like Walter, feels completely lost and alone? While there is only one way to a soul's Redemption, there are many ways people in your family need to be redeemed and find freedom to experience life.

ON THE LOOK-OUT

In almost every movie, directors and producers make a few mistakes, and those mistakes are often quite humorous. Look for these goofs in *Secondhand Lions*:

- Canadian geese speaking a foreign language
- The family visits Hub in the hospital

TEST YOUR TEXAS TRIVIA

1. State flower
   _Bluebonnet
   _Daisy
   _West Indian Lilac
2. State tree
   _Apple
   _Cherry
   _Pecan
3. State pepper
   _Jalapeño
   _Red bell pepper
   _Poblano pepper
4. State vegetable
   _Butternut squash
   _Corn on the cob
   _Sweet onion
5. State dance
   _Macarena
   _Square dance
   _Texas waltz

ROLL 'EM

Show *Secondhand Lions.* Following the movie, serve dessert and discuss ideas from the Prologue.

FUN FACTS

Haley Joel Osment was attacked by the pig during filming. The lion had numerous trainers and handlers, but no one thought the pig might be a menace.

The doctor at the hospital who told the family that Hub had checked out actually is Haley Joel Osment's father.

The giraffe's name was Kelsey.

On the special features side of the DVD, go to the deleted scenes section. While at the top of the list, press the "up" button on your remote control and a star will appear and be highlighted. Press the "Okay" button and a clip of outtakes will come on showing all of the filmmakers' attempts at trying to put the rooster on the pig.

THE PROLOGUE

1. What did you think about the movie? Who were the major characters?
2. What were some of the primary themes?
3. Describe the relationship between Walter and his uncles at the beginning of the movie and at the end of the movie. What was it that created the difference? How did they form a lasting connection? Why did they need that connection?
4. Name some of the adults you feel most connected to. These could be family, close friends, business associates. What is it that creates this connection, this bond between you?

And let us be concerned about one another in order to promote love and good works, not staying away from our meetings, as some habitually do, but encouraging each other, and all the more as you see the day drawing near.

HEBREWS 10:24-25

REFLECTION

1. What scenes from *Secondhand Lions* made an impact on you and why?

2. How did each of the characters need to find redemption in their lives? Walter? His mom? Garth? Hub?

CLIP #1: *Walter Runs*
Chapter 5: ***She Lied . . . Again*** *(start @ beginning, end @ 2:27)*

1. Walter was in desperate need for redemption. Why? What in Walter's life needed to be redeemed?

2. How would you describe the two uncles here? What were some of their obvious differences?

3. Read Isaiah 42:13 and Matthew 23:37 below. What are some of the Christlike characteristics of Hub and Garth at this point? How do each represent different aspects of God?

GARTH: Planning your next move? Where you figure on going?

WALTER: Here. Area code 406. Montana.

GARTH: How come you're not heading to Fort Worth where your momma is?

WALTER: She's not there. She lied . . . again.

GARTH: Listen, kid, we know you got your heart set on going to Montana, but it's late. Hub, help me out here. . . . We got better maps than that one at the house, right, Hub?

HUB: Yeah, a man needs a good map, that's for sure.

WALTER: I've been to the orphan home before. I don't want to go back.

HUB: It ain't our fault you got a lousy mother.

The LORD advances like a warrior; He stirs up His zeal like a soldier.
He shouts, He roars aloud, He prevails over His enemies.
ISAIAH 42:13

"Jerusalem! Jerusalem! Murderer of prophets! Killer of the ones who brought you God's news! How often I've ached to embrace your children, the way a hen gathers her chicks under her wings, and you wouldn't let me."
MATTHEW 23:37 (MSG)

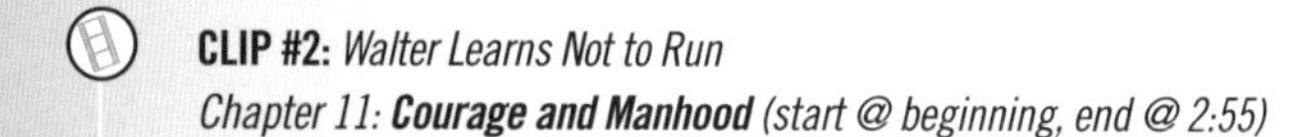

CLIP #2: *Walter Learns Not to Run*
Chapter 11: ***Courage and Manhood*** *(start @ beginning, end @ 2:55)*

---

4. What additional characteristics of these two uncles do you learn about here?

5. What is it about these two men that needs redemption? How has each been drawn into the smaller stories of the enemy's schemes? How do you think Hub has bought into the lie that he is a worn out, secondhand lion?

6. How many "secondhand lions" are in this story? What are the similarities between the real lion and the uncles?

7. How do you think redemption becomes realized through Hub? Would you consider him a good role model? Why or why not?

> The Lord is a warrior; Yahweh is His name.
> **EXODUS 15:3**

CLIP #3: *Walter Becomes the Teacher*
Chapter 14: ***Truth and Belief*** *(start @ 5:08, end @ 8:00)*

---

8. Hub's life is redeemed—transformed by a 14-year-old boy. What did Hub learn about life, particularly if Philippians 4:8 is taken into account? What did Walter give to Hub that changed him forever? How was the Villain defeated and Hub forever changed?

> Whatever is true, whatever is honorable, whatever is just, whatever is pure, whatever is lovely, whatever is commendable—if there is any moral excellence and if there is any praise—dwell on these things.
> **PHILIPPIANS 4:8**

GARTH: All your life, you've never been frightened of anything. So what's eating at you now? Getting old? Dying? What then?

HUB: Being useless. When we were young there was always a reason; there was a point. Things made sense. Now there's no point to anything. So what do we do? We garden. We outlived our time, brother.

HUB: People are basically good; that honor, courage, and virtue mean everything; that power and money, money and power mean nothing; that good always triumphs over evil. And I want you to remember this, that love . . . true love never dies. You remember that, boy. You remember that. . . . A man should believe in those things because those are the things worth believing in.

WALTER: I can't be a good man until you give me the rest of the speech, right? So you need to stick around until I'm old enough to hear the whole thing. . . .

HUB: You won't be living here then.

WALTER: You're my uncle. I need you to stick around and be my uncle. What about Uncle Garth? He needs you. What about the dogs and the pig, and the lion? We all need you. I need you. . .

9. What does Walter teach us about giving to others?

CLIP #4: *Walter Finds the Courage of a Lion*
Chapter 17: ***A Real Lion*** *(start @ beginning, end @ 1:25)*

10. Here we meet another villain in the story. Like the larger Villain, he mixes a little truth with his lies, but ultimately is revealed for the liar he is. The villain (Stan) in *Secondhand Lions* tries to make Walter question the goodness of his uncles. How is this similar to how the Villain attacks our lives? (EXP-71)

STAN: Getting warmer, huh?

WALTER: No, let go!

STAN (hits Walter in the stomach): Let's you and me get something straight. We can be friends or we can be enemies. I've had a run of crummy luck lately. I know some bad people who want to cause a lot of trouble for me. I need that money and I know it's close. So what's it gonna be, pal? Friends or enemies?

WALTER: Defend yourself. (kicks Stan, gets free, and runs)

11. In this scene, we really see two "lions." One, like our Heavenly Father (Rev. 5:5), was faithful and decisive when it came to protecting her "cub," giving her life for him. The other transformed "lion," Walter, saved and redeemed the lives of his two uncles. How did Walter make a difference in their lives?

> Look! The Lion from the tribe of Judah,
> the Root of David, has been victorious.
> **REVELATION 5:5**

12. In the beginning of the movie, Walter was a frightened, intimidated 14- year-old. Here, we see him stand up to a much bigger aggressor, and later to his mother. Read the passages below. How can we explain the transformation in Walter's life? (EXP-71)

> The LORD your God is among you, a warrior who saves. He will rejoice over you with gladness. He will bring you quietness with His love. He will delight in you with shouts of joy."
> **ZEPHANIAH 3:17**

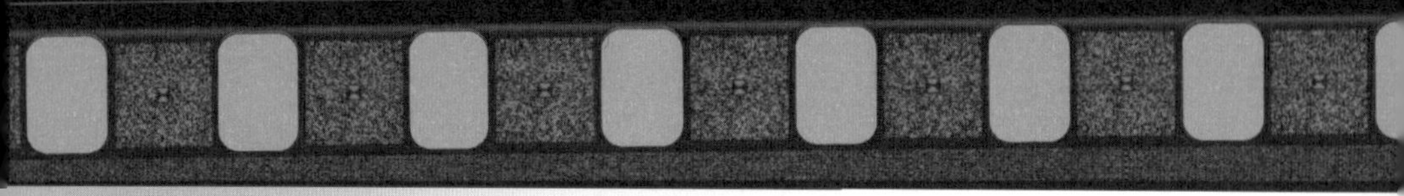

SHERIFF: Here. I found their will.

WALTER: "The kid gets it all. Just plant us in the garden with the stupid lion."

CLIP #5: *The Kid Gets It All*
Chapter 20: ***Real Legends*** *(start @ beginning, end @ 2:55)*

13. Just like Act IV of the Larger Story ends us for us, so, too, does *Secondhand Lions* end for Walter: "the kid gets it all." How is the quote below similar to 1 Corinthians 2:9? (EXP-72)

SHERIFF: Here. I found their will.

WALTER: "The kid gets it all. Just plant us in the garden with the stupid lion."

Long, long ago he decided to adopt us into his family through
Jesus Christ. (What pleasure he took in planning this!)
EPHESIANS 1:5 (MSG)

... but just as it is written,
"Things which eye has not seen and ear has not heard,
and which have not entered the heart of man,
all that God has prepared for those who love him."
1 CORINTHIANS 2:9 (NAS)

[18]The building material of its wall was jasper, and the city was pure gold like clear glass. [19]The foundations of the city wall were adorned with every kind of precious stone ...[20]The 12 gates are 12 pearls; each individual gate was made of a single pearl. The broad street of the city was pure gold, like transparent glass.
REVELATION 21:18-20

GOING VERTICAL

Tonight, pray that you won't forget "Walter"—teenagers and young adults who seem lost and need redemption. If you know someone who needs a "Garth" or a "Hub," pray for the wisdom and opportunity for you to be able to give your "what every person needs to know" speech about God's true Redemption.

Pray that you won't forget "Hub" or "Garth"—older folks who seem isolated and alone, who simply watch the clock, waiting for the day to hurry up and end. Is there someone you know who is waiting for "Walter" to pull up in his driveway to give is "We all need you" speech? Pray for the strength of a lion these days to make a difference in your world.

AN UNFINISHED LIFE

AN UNFINISHED LIFE

DINNER AND A MOVIE — WEEK 1

An Unfinished Life (2005)
Directed by Lasse Hallstrom
Writing credits: Mark Spragg and Virginia Korus Spragg
Starring: Robert Redford, Jennifer Lopez, Morgan Freeman, Josh Lucas
MPAA: Rated PG-13 for some violence including domestic abuse and language
Runtime: 107 minutes

SETTING THE STAGE

THE BUZZ

"To see a quiet, thoughtful film like this is almost a relief. . . .
It isn't fast, it isn't flashy, but in the hands of Freeman and Redford, it's got depth."

JOSHUA TYLER, CINEMABLEND.COM

"With its gorgeous locations (the farmstead, especially) contributing much to this delicious spectacle, *An Unfinished Life* is highly satisfying work."

DORIS TOUMARKINE, FILM JOURNAL INTERNATIONAL

THE STORY

In this story, a bitter rancher, Einar Gilkyson (Redford), grieves long after the death of his adult son in a car accident. But when the 11-year-old granddaughter he never knew existed suddenly enters his life, love and tenderness slowly begin again to grow. *An Unfinished Life* explores several themes, with the healing power of forgiveness being the most important. The film's principal conflict is between Einar and his estranged daughter-in-law, Jean (Lopez), both of whom haven't communicated since the untimely death of the young man over a decade ago. Einar can't forgive Jean for causing the accident that took his son's life. After being physically abused by a tempestuous boyfriend one too many times, Jean and her daughter leave home and end up on Einar's Wyoming doorstep, where they are not welcome at first. Einar's best friend, Mitch, however, also lives on the ranch, and he welcomes them eagerly. With the help of his best friend and his daughter-in-law, Einar is forced to re-examine his life, and his family finds the redemption they have needed for years.

THE MENU

The menu items selected to accompany *An Unfinished Life* are closely associated with the film's setting, the West. Consider preparing the recipes found in the

TEST YOUR BEAR TRIVIA

1. What fictional bear was found in a train station and named after that station?
   _Grand Central Bear
   _Paddington Bear
   _Choo Choo bear
2. Smokey the Bear was the symbol of the US Forest Service for many years. He was a real bear. What species was he?
   _Brown Bear
   _American Black Bear
   _Sun Bear
3. What is the name of the Wacka-Wacka bear from the Muppets?
   _Fozzie
   _Wally
   _Miss Piggy Bear
4. The late coach Bear Bryant led which college football team?
   _Notre Dame
   _Florida State
   _Alabama
5. In the TV show MASH, what was Radar's teddy bear's name?
   _Rosie
   _Theodore Akin
   _He didn't have a name

Experience Guide, or use your own creativity to make your movie and dinner nights special for your group. The suggested menu for this session includes:

WESTERN OMELET PIE

FRUIT SALSA

WYOMING WHOPPER COOKIES

BEFORE STEPPING INTO ANOTHER WORLD ...

- Ask God to speak to you and reveal more of his heart to you in this time.
- Pay attention to what moves you. Be very aware of those moments during which you "feel" something more.
- Take special note of how you feel during specific scenes.
- As you step into the world of *An Unfinished Life*, be ready to encounter a world in which characters are being held hostage by their pain and loss. Be sensitive to signs of the enemy. Who is the real villain?

ROLL 'EM

Show *An Unfinished Life.* Remember that this movie is rated PG-13 for violence and language.

THE PROLOGUE

1. This movie is about injured, wounded, and hurting people—and the redemption they ultimately find. What was your worst injury as a child—a broken bone, stitches, really bad sunburn? Have fun with this. Ask everyone to give an answer.

2. When everyone has shared, ask two or three of the participants: So how long did it take for the pain to go away and your injury to heal?

3. Sometimes our injuries don't heal so quickly. Sometimes we don't or can't let them heal. And we need help. Oftentimes this healing of injury only comes through a significant battle with forgiveness. During Jesus' Sermon on the Mount, He said, "For if you forgive people their wrongdoing, your heavenly Father will forgive you as well. But if you don't forgive people, your Father will not forgive your wrongdoing" (HCSB). How literally do you think we should take His statement here?

Read the verse below and discuss the ways bitterness, anger, and wrath may be removed from you. Close by asking God to reveal these ways to you in the interim before the next get-together.

> All bitterness, anger and wrath, insult and slander must be removed from you, **along with all wickedness. And** be kind and compassionate to one another, forgiving one another, just as God also forgave you in Christ.
>
> **EPHESIANS 4:31-32**

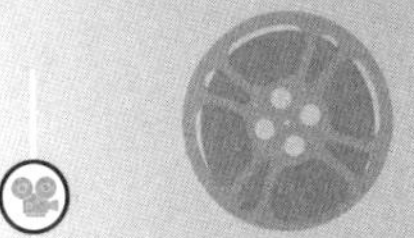

REFLECTION

1. Can you remember who the characters were, the wounds they sustained, and the conflict they dealt with as a result?

2. Who do you think was hurt the worst, and why?

3. Why open the movie with the bear? Notice how he is woven throughout this story. Discuss what the bear represents. How did Jesus handle the wildness and unpredictability of life (cross)?

JEAN GILKYSON: Griffin flipped a coin and I lost. So I was the one who was driving. It was 3 o'clock in the morning and we were both tired. We wanted to make it down to the rodeo in Great Falls.

CLIP #1: *Jean's Confession*
Chapter 11: ***I Killed Griffin***

JEAN GILKYSON: I killed him, Einar. Is that what you wanna hear? It wasn't the change in our pockets, or the weak coffee, or the rain. It was me. I fell asleep and I flipped the car six times. I killed Griffin. You have no argument from me. You think it's something I forget? You think that I'm not sick with it, that I hate my life? But I tried to keep living, and you haven't. Is that why you hate me so much? You know, you act like I killed you the day Griffin died.

---

1. Whom did Jean refuse to forgive? How did Jean handle her pain?

2. Read Hebrews 12:15. What does this verse tell us about the pitfalls of not unforgiving? How did not forgiving affect Einar and Jean?

> See to it that no one falls short of the grace of God
> and that no root of bitterness springs up,
> causing trouble and by it, defiling many.
> HEBREWS 12:15

CLIP #2: *Einar's Anger Surfaces*
Chapter 7: ***Accidents***

EINAR: Tell your kid to come down out of that tree.

JEAN: (breaks a plate) I'm sorry.

EINAR: You're sorry, huh? Well, that's just fine then.

JEAN: I'll buy you a new one.

EINAR: Oh, just that easy? Maybe I liked that plate. In fact, maybe that was my favorite . . . plate.

JEAN: It's just a plate.

EINAR: That's it, huh? Did it ever occur to you that not everything can be replaced?

3. Jean thinks it is only a plate. Discuss what this angry outburst is really about for Einar?

4. Not just in this scene, but throughout most of the film, why was Einar so angry? What was preventing him from letting go of his bitterness? Who were the persons he needed to forgive?

5. In *An Unfinished Life*, what is in need of redemption? What is standing in the way?

CLIP #3: *The Villains*
Chapter 1: ***We're Going to Wyoming***

GARY: I don't know what happened. It's like a red mist or something comes over me and I . . . but I feel like you back me up in a corner and I . . . you do that and I hate it when I'm like that.

GRIFF: You promised—if it happened again—you promised.

6. In a broad sense, who are the villains in the movie . . .Gary? Jean? Einar? The sense of guilt/unforgiveness?

7. An unforgiving spirit was possibly the greatest villain in the story. How can unforgiveness act as a villain in our lives?

8. Read 1 Peter 5:8 below. Who is the ultimate Villain—the one trying to control each of these characters' lives—in this and every story? How do you see him at work? (EXP-79)

Be sober! Be on the alert! Your adversary the Devil is prowling around like a roaring lion, looking for anyone he can devour.
1 PETER 5:8

CLIP #4: *Mitch Deals with His Anger*
Chapter 13: ***Mitch's Emergency***

EINAR: How you doin'?

MITCH: You can't just leave him there, Einar. We walked into his business. He was just doing what bears do. We can't punish him for that. Got to let him go, Einar. Get him out of that cage.

EINAR: Don't you lie here and think I could do that.

MITCH: You know I could get myself shaved in the morning, all the way dressed, too. Could probably manage to stick myself with one of those syringes if it came to it. But what I can't do is continue to lie here every day and watch you mourn for a life you think you should have had. There are people everywhere who think they got dealt a bad hand, Einar.

9. Why was Mitch so insistent here that they had to let the bear go? What does the bear represent? What did the cage represent? What began finally to break in Einar's heart once he released Mitch's "bear"?

10. Take note of the juxtaposition between how Einar and Jean handle their pain and need to forgive versus the way Mitch handles forgiving both the bear and Einar for being drunk. Read Hebrews 12:1-2 and think about how the principles in these verses give meaning to the characters in the movie. (EXP-80)

[1]Therefore since we also have such a large cloud of witnesses surrounding us, let us lay aside every weight and the sin that so easily ensnares us, and run with endurance the race that lies before us, [2]keeping our eyes on Jesus, the source and perfecter of our faith, who for the joy that lay before Him endured a cross and despised the shame, and has sat down at the right hand of God's throne.

HEBREWS 12:1-2

11. In what ways does Mitch live life in a way similar to the model of Jesus given in Hebrews 12:2?

CLIP #5: *Einar and Mitch Can Relax*
Chapter 18: ***Conclusion and Credits***

EINAR: Think it might rain today.

MITCH: Naw, it's gonna stay warm.

EINAR: I didn't say anything about the temperature. I said it might rain.

MITCH: Would you bury me next to Griffin?

EINAR: Don't you think you oughtta die first?

MITCH: It's gonna happen, you know.

EINAR: Where else do you think I'd bury you? It's where my family lies. You think the dead really care about our lives?

MITCH: Yeah, I think they do. I think they forgive us our sins. I even think it's easy for them.

EINAR: Griff said you had a dream about flying.

MITCH: Yeah. I got so high, Einar. I could see where the blue turns to black. From up there, you can see all there is. And it looked like there was a reason for everything.

12. What motivation or perspective did Mitch seem to have that freed him to forgive and release his wounds?

13. What significant confession does Einar share with Jean in the hospital?

14. Forgiveness brought redemption to each of these characters' lives, and broke the stronghold which Satan had created. What were some of the effects of forgiveness in the lives of the characters in the movie?

For although we are walking in the flesh, we do not wage war in a fleshly way, since the weapons of our warfare are not fleshly, but are powerful through God for the demolition of strongholds. We demolish arguments and every high-minded thing that is raised up against the knowledge of God, taking every thought captive to the obedience of Christ.
2 CORINTHIANS 10:3-5

15. If forgiveness is a key weapon (2 Cor. 10), what is the relationship between "strongholds" and "redemption"? (EXP-81)

16. In 2 Corinthians 10:4-5, Paul implies we all have strongholds. Can you identify any of Satan's strongholds or fortresses that exist in your life?

17. How might strongholds like resentment, self-pity, envy, hostility, unhealed wounds, unforgiveness, and jealousy aid the real villain in your life? How might the Villain keep you from experiencing redemption and freedom?

GOING VERTICAL

How does the Villain attack your life? We are all in need of freedom from guilt, pain, anxiety, grief, and bitterness. God has given us an incredible arsenal of ways to fight the Villain and forgiveness is one of those weapons. As you go vertical to close tonight's meeting take these questions to God.

- God, are there areas of unforgiveness in my life? Is there an offense that needs my forgiveness? Is there an offense for which I need to be forgiven?
- How is my unforgiveness keeping me captive?

Take these questions to your heart.

- Am I willing to utilize the awesome spiritual weapon of forgiveness against the real Villain?
- If not, then why do I yield? If yes, then how will I deploy it?

NOTES

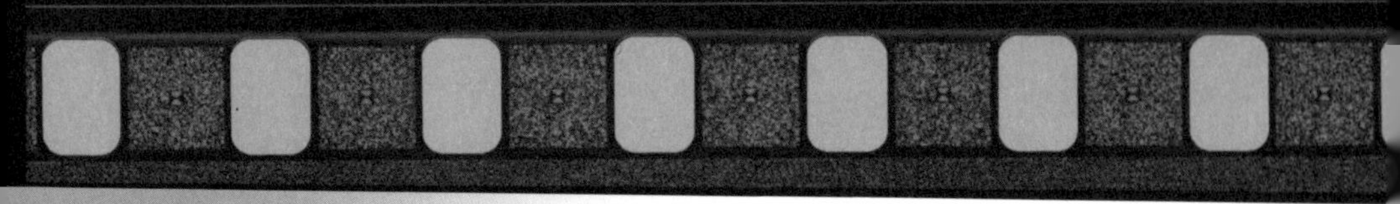

NOTES

SEABISCUIT

TEST YOUR SEABISCUIT IQ

1. What make of cars did Charles Howard sell at his dealership?
   _Ford
   _Buick
   _Rolls-Royce

2. How many times was Red seriously injured while riding?
   _1
   _5
   _3
   _2

3. What famous horse was Seabiscuit a descendant of?
   _Man o' War
   _Phar Lap
   _Omaha
   _Affirmed

4. Where did Seabiscuit and War Admiral race?
   _Kentucky
   _Santa Anita
   _Saratoga
   _Pimlico

SEABISCUIT

DINNER AND A MOVIE — WEEK 1

Seabiscuit (2003)
Directed by Gary Ross
Writing credits: Laura Hillenbrand (novel); Gary Ross (screenplay)
Starring: Toby Maguire, Jeff Bridges, and Chris Cooper
MPAA: Rated PG-13 for some sexual situations and violent sports-related images
Runtime: 141 min

SETTING THE STAGE

THE BUZZ

"This is the tale about a horse that is too small, a jockey who is too big, a trainer who is too old, and the owner who chooses not to notice. It's about the little guy who doesn't know he's little. It's a beautifully crafted film, filled with richness and vibrancy, with a story that pierces the heart."

URBAN CINEFILE CRITICS, URBAN CINEFILE

"*Seabiscuit* is a grand ride. Sleek, beautiful and packed with emotion, not too flashy but full of heart."

JAMES BERADINELLI, REELVIEWS

THE STORY

Based on Laura Hillenbrand's best-selling book of the same name, *Seabiscuit* depicts a racehorse of celebrity status. He was too-small, ill-tempered, and never should have won—yet somehow managed to defeat the greatest racehorses of his day.

Our first glimpse of this great horse shows us a lethargic, overweight, and unmanageable animal dumped by his first trainer, Sunny Fitzsimmons. Then we follow his genuinely inspiring rise to world fame. Along the way, we are privileged to see the dramatic backstory behind Seabiscuit's fame. We also meet the three men who plucked "The Biscuit" from mediocrity and nurtured him to greatness.

First is Seabiscuit's wealthy owner, Charles Howard. Howard was a bicycle repairman who gambled on the success of the automobile, rose to wealth, and was then hit by tragedy. He turned to horse racing as a diversion from grief. Second we see the trainer, Tom Smith, who was a cowboy with a natural instinct for horse training. As he was bringing a crippled horse back to health, he was spotted by Howard and hired to train and nurture Seabiscuit into a powerhouse. Third, there is the tragic, accident-prone jockey, Johnny "Red" Pollard. Red was a middle-class kid whose family went bankrupt during the Depression. Talented but insecure, he was forced into jockeying to earn his keep.

THE MENU

The menu items selected to accompany Seabiscuit are closely associated with a day at the races. Some race fans have been known to serve this exact menu every first Saturday in May. Consider preparing the recipes found in the Experience Guide, or use your own creativity to make your movie and dinner nights special for your group.

SPICED MUSTARD-GLAZED HAM

GREEN BEANS WITH LEMON

CORN PUDDING

DERBY PIE

BEFORE STEPPING INTO ANOTHER WORLD …

- Ask God to speak to you and reveal more of his heart to you in this time.
- Pay attention to what moves you. Be very aware of those moments during which you "feel' something more.
- Take special note of how you feel during specific scenes.
- As you watch *Seabiscuit*, think about how God uses people in our lives to take us on a journey into redemptive healing.

ON THE LOOK-OUT

In almost every movie, directors and producers make a few mistakes, and those mistakes are often quite humorous. Look for these goofs in *Seabiscuit*:

- Look at the montage of still photographs purporting to show the first year of the Great Depression.
- During Seabiscuit's Santa Anita Handicap win, he is shown to be running dead last early in the race. But this isn't correct.

THE PROLOGUE

1. Think about your relationships—all of them—and the various communities you move in and out of during a week. Describe these relationships and communities.

2. What are some movies that come to mind when you think about "community"?

3. What makes these communities memorable?

4. How would you define the term "redemptive community"? How do you think "redemptive community" is different from "community"?

5. Describe a time when God worked through someone else to redeem an event, a particular mess, or something else in your life.

REFLECTION

1. Which scenes in *Seabiscuit* impacted you the most? Why?

2. What single thread wove itself through all of the characters' lives?

3. In *Seabiscuit* we find a group of people (and an animal) coming together to achieve a specific goal. Who were they? How were they alike? What was their bond?

4. How was each of these characters wounded? What different ways did each character deal with or live out his wounds?

5. What does Isaiah 61:1-2 imply that we all need?

> [1]The Spirit of the LORD God is on Me, because the LORD has anointed Me to bring good news to the poor. He has sent Me to heal the brokenhearted, [2]to proclaim liberty to the captives, and freedom to the prisoners; to proclaim the year of the LORD's favor, and the day of our God's vengeance; to comfort all who mourn
>
> ISAIAH 61:1-2

NARRATOR: The first time he saw Seabiscuit, the colt was walking through the fog at 5:00 in the morning. Smith would say later that the horse looked right through him, as if to say, "What are you looking at? Who do you think you are?" . . . They made him a training partner to better horses, forcing him to lose head-to-head duels to boost the confidence of the other animal. Soon he grew as bitter and angry as his sire Hard Tack had been. He was sold for the rock bottom price of $2,000. And, of course, it all made sense. . . . When they finally did race him, he did just what they had trained him to do. He lost.

CLIP #1: *Seabiscuit's History*
Chapter 9: (Start @ 46:00 and end @ 47:05)

1. How do the characters' similarities in this movie mirror what we oftentimes see today in people's lives?

2. How does Seabiscuit's story actually parallel Red's story?

CLIP #2: *You Don't Throw a Whole Life Away*
Chapter 8: (Start @ beginning and end @ 42:00)

3. Wounds can be handled in many ways. Read Jeremiah 6:14. What does this verse say about the way we sometimes handle the wounds of others? Why is God so critical of us in Jeremiah 6:14? (EXP-89)

They have treated My people's brokenness superficially, claiming:
Peace, peace, when there is no peace.
JEREMIAH 6:14

CLIP #3: *He Can Do Great Things*
Chapter 7: (Start @ 1:07:55 and end @ 1:08:48)

NARRATOR: In the end, it wasn't the dams or the roads or the bridges or the parks. Or the tunnels or the thousands of other public projects that were built in those years. It was more invisible than that. Men who were broken only a year before suddenly felt restored. Men who'd been shattered suddenly found their voice.

CHARLES: Well, I just think this horse has a lot of heart. He may have been down, but he wasn't out. He may have lost a few, but he didn't let it get to him. We could all learn a lick or two from this little guy. Oh, and by the way, he doesn't know he's little. He thinks he's the biggest horse out there. . . . See, sometimes when the little guy, he doesn't know he's a little guy, he can do great big things.

CHARLES: Who's that?

MAN: Huh? Oh, he's a crackpot. Lives alone in the bushes.

CHARLES: What's he do?

MAN: I don't know. He used to be a trainer, farrier. Now he just looks after that horse. Come on. Let's look at another barn.

(later)

TOM: Howdy.

CHARLES: Hello. (referring to a horse) Will he get better?

TOM: Already is . . . a little.

CHARLES: Will he race?

TOM: No. Not that one.

CHARLES: So why are you fixing him?

TOM: 'Cause I can. Every horse is good for somethin'. He could be a cart horse or a lead pony. And he's still nice to look at. You know, you don't throw a whole life away just 'cause he's banged up a little.

4. As the movie progressed, what became the characters' bond (beyond their brokenness)? How did they experience redemption?

5. In the Christian community, how successful do you think the church is at helping people achieve this kind of personal redemption? Why? Can you share a brief example?

6. How was their connection—their bond of community—important to each other's success?

7. Read Mark 3:13-14 below. What was the first reason given for Jesus' calling of The Twelve? Talk a little about the "be-with" factor. (EXP-90)

Then He went up the mountain and summoned those He wanted, and they came to Him. He also appointed 12—He also named them apostles—*to be with Him* to send them out to preach, and to have authority to drive out demons.

MARK 3:13-14 (Italic Added for Emphasis)

CLIP #4: *He Fixed Us*
Chapter 7: (Start @ 2:11:00 and end @ 2:12:10)

RED: You know, everybody thinks we found this broken-down horse and fixed him, but we didn't. He fixed us. Every one of us. And I guess, in a way, we kind of fixed each other, too.

8. Why do you suppose in James 5:16 God encourages us to tell our stories to one another and even reveal our sins (secrets)?

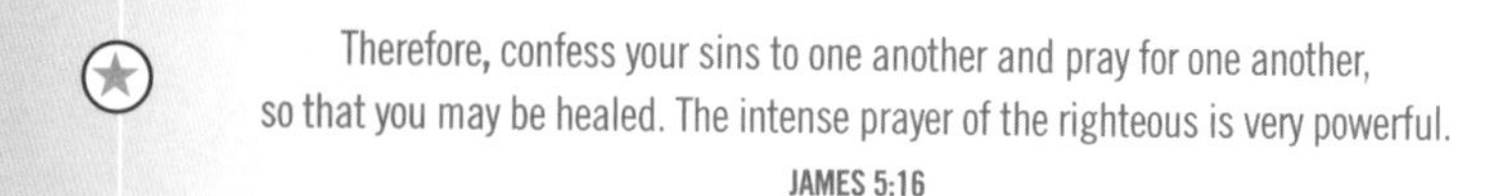

Therefore, confess your sins to one another and pray for one another, so that you may be healed. The intense prayer of the righteous is very powerful.

JAMES 5:16

9. Read Proverbs 20:5 below. How does the principle of asking clarifying questions and seeking to be discerning in one another's lives apply to the healing process? How is it demonstrated in this movie?

CHARLES: Son, what are you so angry about?

Counsel in a man's heart is deep water;
but a man of understanding draws it up.

PROVERBS 20:5

10. Read 1 Peter 4:8. From the movie, can you remember scenes where empathy (deep love) played a critical role in each of these folk's redemptive journey? How do these scenes help us to understand the 1 Peter passage?

Above all, keep your love for one another at full strength,
since love covers a multitude of sins.

1 PETER 4:8

11. Typically when we are moved by a story, it is because it is either borrowing from the larger story of life, from our own story, or both. Which is it for you? What part of this movie made you stop and think? Why do you think this is the case?

GOING VERTICAL

Tom says, "You don't throw a whole life away just 'cause he's banged up a little." *Seabiscuit* implies rather openly that we're all banged up a little, yet all worth saving. In fact, our wounds can make us beautiful in the light of God's redemptive story. Jesus says that He came to give us a crown of beauty instead of ashes (Is. 61:3; Luke 4:18-19). This Connecting the Dots experience reveals the power of community as God fulfills His promise of ultimate redemption. As you close this study of redemption pray in the following way.

- Help us live and experience real redemptive community.
- God, we want and need more of You. Just like all of the characters in the story, we're banged up.
- Give us courage to tell our stories–our true stories. Give us the strength to share our messes so you can work through our community.
- Instill in us a passion that accepts nothing less than true redemptive community.

NOTES

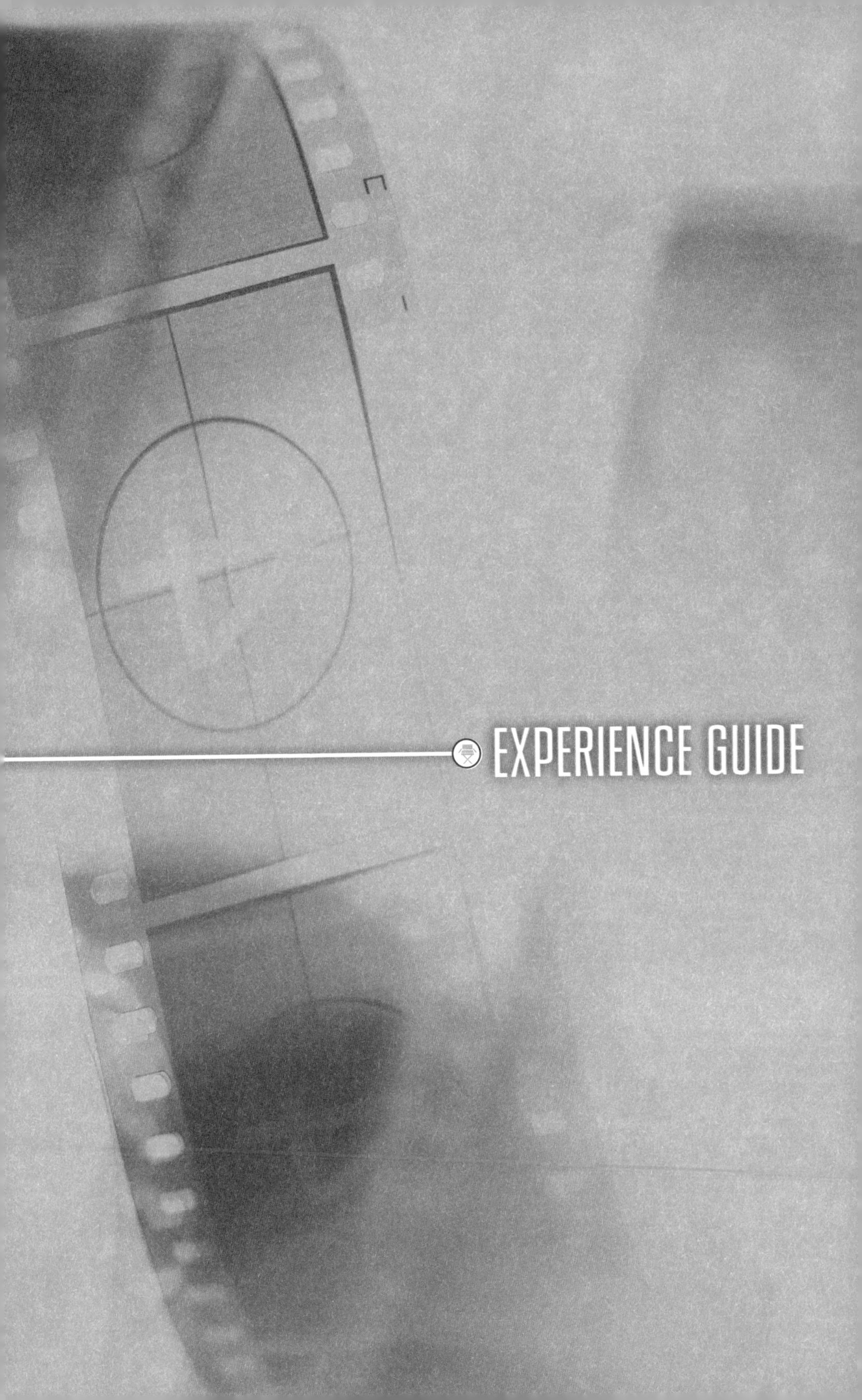

EXPERIENCE GUIDE

THE COUNT OF MONTE CRISTO

DINNER AND A MOVIE WEEK 1

GETTING STARTED

1. Rent *The Count of Monte Cristo*
2. Create decorating ideas
3. Review the dinner menu

SETTING THE STAGE

DÉCOR

For tonight's decorations, you may wish to decorate the table to resemble a small French bistro. Simple decorations could include a white tablecloth, a few Perrier bottles with candles and/or French flags, sparkling cider and a cheese tray, a cut out fleur de lis used on place mats or as napkin rings. You also may want to play some traditional French music softly as the participants gather or during the meal. Edith Piaf is a traditional French musician and singer, and her music can be found in many music shops and web sites such as iTunes.

DINNER

Discuss dinner responsibilities with group members at least a week in advance of this dinner and a movie night. As an added convenience for members, we have posted the recipes at www.SerendipityHouse.com.

Monte Cristo Sandwiches

1/2 cup mayonnaise
1/4 tsp. ground nutmeg
1/8 tsp. freshly ground pepper
12 slices white bread, crusts removed
6 slices Swiss cheese
6 slices cooked ham
6 slices cooked chicken
2 eggs
1/2 cup milk

In a small bowl, combine mayonnaise, nutmeg, and pepper; spread on one side of each bread slice. Layer cheese, ham and chicken on 6 bread slices; top with remaining bread, mayonnaise sides down. Cut sandwiches diagonally into quarters. In small bowl, beat together eggs and milk; dip sandwich quarters into egg mixture. Cook on preheated greased griddle or in skillet, turning once, 4 to 5 minutes or until browned and heated through. Sprinkle cooled sandwiches with powdered sugar and serve with raspberry preserves.

Cassoulet

1/2 lb. sausage
1 small onion, sliced
1 clove garlic, minced
1 1/2 cups cubed cooked ham
1 tablespoon parsley
1/4 cup white wine
2-15 oz. cans navy beans, undrained
1 bay leaf

In a skillet, cook sausage, onion, and garlic until sausage is lightly browned and onion is tender. Drain off fat. Add remaining ingredients and pour into a greased 1 1/2 quart casserole. Bake, covered, in a 325° oven for 45 minutes. Uncover and bake 45 minutes more, stirring occasionally. Remove bay leaf. Serve in bowls.

Raspberry Trifle

---

1 loaf (10 3/4 ounces) frozen pound cake
1 1/2 cups whipping cream
3/4 cups sugar
2 pkgs (8 oz each) cream cheese, softened
2 teaspoons lemon juice
2 teaspoons vanilla extract
2 pkgs (10 ounces each) frozen sweetened raspberries, thawed (unsweetened can be substituted)
2 tablespoons cocoa powder
Fresh raspberries, optional (for garnish)

Slice cake into 18-20 slices about 1/2" thick; set aside. In a mixing bowl, beat cream with 1/4 cup sugar until stiff peaks form. In another bowl, beat cream cheese, lemon juice, vanilla, and the remaining sugar. Fold in 2 cups of the whipped cream; set remaining whipped cream aside for topping. Drain raspberries, reserving juice; set berries aside. Line the bottom of a 3-quart glass bowl with a third of the cake slices. Drizzle with some of the raspberry juice. Spread with a fourth of the cream cheese mixture. Sift a fourth of the cocoa over the top. Sprinkle with a third of the berries. Repeat layers twice. Top with the remaining cream cheese mixture, whipped cream, and sifted cocoa. Cover and refrigerate for 4 hours or overnight. Garnish with fresh raspberries if desired.

ON THE LOOK-OUT

Here are the answers to the hints given earlier. You may want to provide a prize for the person who finds all three of these goofs.

- Overhead power lines and a radio communications tower

  During the last sword fight in the wheat field, large overhead power lines are clearly visible in the valley. A radio communications tower is also visible next to the building, off in the distance.

- Eye color for a major character

  Edmond's eye color changes from brown to blue and back to brown throughout the movie.

- A blue object along the shoreline

  When Dantes runs along the shoreline, a blue object can be seen in the background. This must be a crew member because none of the smugglers are wearing blue.

TRIVIA ANSWERS

1. 20
2. A city in eastern France
3. Mustard
4. True
5. Louis XVI

THE PROLOGUE

Before the meeting, ask four or five members of the group to be prepared to retell briefly the story of Joseph from Genesis 37:1—45:15. They will need to coordinate who will share which parts of the story. As dessert is served, ask these members to tell the story. Then ask these members to serve as an informal panel to discuss some of the following questions:

CONNECTING THE DOTS — WEEK 2

GETTING STARTED

- Review the Bible study questions and Scripture references.
- Review the clips identified in the Bible study content. You'll want to be able to find these clips quickly and have a good handle on how they're used. Here are the Bible study clips from *The Count of Monte Cristo* in the order they'll be used during your meeting:

1. Characters Revealed
   Chapter 3: ***The New Captain*** (start @ beginning and end @ 4:42)
2. A Larger Story
   Chapter 25: ***Villefort*** (start @ :55 and end @ 4:30)
3. He Sees Everything
   Chapter 7: ***Chateau d'If*** (start @ 2:15 and end at 3:30)
4. Edmond the Student
   Chapter 11: ***Neglect Becomes Our Ally*** (start @ 2:55 and end @ scene 12, 2:20)
5. God Is in Everything
   Chapter 26: ***Mercedes and Edmond*** (start @ beginning and end @ 2:30)

Prior to the Bible study we recommend a quick review of the movie. It will also add to the experience to show the movie trailer. Many times the theatrical trailer will be included on the DVD.

BIBLE STUDY GUIDE

REFLECTIONS

1. During our last meeting we watched *The Count of Monte Cristo.* Were there any scenes that impacted you—either made you feel passionately emotional or left you with a "lump in your throat"? Explain.

2. What was this movie about? What were the plots and subplots and themes?

3. In *The Count of Monte Cristo* we are introduced to several characters. Who were they and what were their roles?

   Edmond . . . . Main character, hero, redeemed
   Mondego . . . . His friend and betrayer
   Danglar . . . . First mate of the ship, betrayer
   Mercedes . . . . The beauty, redeemed
   Villefort . . . . Chief Magistrate (villain, sent Edmond to prison)
   Dorleac . . . . Prison warden (villain)
   Priest . . . . Prisoner, teacher, redeemer figure
   Jacopo . . . . Guardian angel

4. Which of these characters did you identify with the most? Why?

   Opinion question—affirm all answers. Obviously, this movie is about the suffering of Edmond Dantes.

5. Describe the extent and levels of Edmund's suffering.

   Betrayal of friends and colleagues
   Loss of family
   Loss of Mercedes
   Injustice
   Loss of future
   Loss of career as a captain
   Loneliness
   Beatings at the prison

6. If you were Edmond, which of these would have hurt you the most?

7. Do you think Edmond did anything to contribute to the events that led to his imprisonment and injustice? *Yes and no. He was naïve concerning friendship. He chose to overlook poor character in his selection of a friend. Additionally, he exposed his love to this character. However, despite these lapses in judgment, nothing he did warranted his plight.*

CLIP #1: *Characters Revealed*
Chapter 3: ***The New Captain*** *(start @ beginning and end @ 4:42)*

MONDEGO (to Mercedes): Make love to me.

MERCEDES. Will you ever give up?

MONDEGO: He doesn't have to know.

MERCEDES: I'd know.

MONDEGO: So would I. It'd be our little secret.

MERCEDES: I don't believe in secrets.

MONDEGO: You think Edmond doesn't have secrets? He does. Ask him.

MERCEDES: I know what you want, Fernand.

MONDEGO: You do!

MERCEDES: Remember when we were kids and Edmond got that whistle for his birthday, and you got a pony? You were so mad Edmond was happier with his whistle than you were with your pony. And I'm not going to be your next whistle. . . .

EDMOND (meeting his friends): Hey! . . .

MONDEGO: Yours is a life truly blessed, Edmond.

EDMOND: You're still the best man.

MONDEGO: I know.

1. Very early in the movie we are introduced to Edmond Dantes and Fernand Mondego. What are they like? How are they different? *Edmond is hopeful, naïve, trusting, a person of integrity and character. Fernand is scheming, duplicitous; he has a dark heart and a brooding temperament.*

   How do you feel about each?

2. Later in the movie Edmond asks Fernand why he turned his back on him and deceived him as a friend. And Fernand answers, "Because you're the son of a clerk, and I'm not supposed to want to be you." What does this quote reveal about Fernand's motivation? *Jealousy and covetousness, and a sinister sense of entitlement.*

3. It is generally held that Isaiah 14:12-15 and Ezekiel 28:12-17 provide the back-story to the Villain and existence of evil in our world. How does Fernand Mondego's character parallel the Villain in the larger story? Like Lucifer, *Fernand was born into privilege and position, yet it wasn't enough. He had to have everything. Villains are frequently born out of jealousy.*

CLIP #2: *A Larger Story*
Chapter 25: ***Villefort*** *(start @ :55 and end @ 4:30)*

COUNT: I was just curious. Why did you tell Countess Mondego 16 years ago that Edmond Dantes had been executed?

VILLEFORT: I don't understand. What on earth are you talking about?

COUNT: It's a perfectly simple question.

VILLEFORT: How do you know these things? You don't understand. Dantes was accepting a letter from Napoleon. That was clearly treason.

COUNT: But we both know he never delivered it. Packing a man off to prison with such knowledge is bad enough. But to tell . . .

VILLEFORT: Your grace, I have no idea what is provoking this perverse discussion.

COUNT: Now I ask myself, "What did my old friend Villefort stand to gain by telling Mercedes that Edmond Dantes is dead?"

4. What were the real reasons for Edmond's suffering and imprisonment? What was going on in France and in Villefort's family? Talk about this subplot. *There were issues at play that Edmond knew nothing about. There was international intrigue because Villefort's father was loyal to Napoleon, and Villefort was ambitious. As a result, a deep conflict and divide surfaced between Villefort and his father.*
5. Read Job 1:6-12. How do these unseen factors that affected Edmond so significantly parallel the unseen elements in Job's life? *Just like Job who had to deal with horrific injustice and suffering due to nothing he did, so too Edmond was at the mercy of events and issues he had nothing to do with.*
6. Was Job at fault for his suffering? Given the back-story seen in Job 1:6-12, talk about circumstances (good or bad) as a legitimate indicator of God's favor or disfavor. *This is one of the most confusing and misunderstood principles in Scripture. Circumstances are an unreliable measure of God's favor or disfavor. Yet this measurement is almost always one of the mistakes made when attempting to interpret life. "When bad things happen," we think, "the problem must relate to an action on my part." Sometimes suffering does come from the consequences of our own decisions. Other times (as Job 1 reveals), there is a larger story at play, and our own experience has nothing to do with the onset of the problem.*

EDMOND DANTES: I don't believe in God.

ABBE FARIA: It doesn't matter. He believes in you.

7. As a result of the injustice and pain he experienced, Edmond denounced God. How did you feel about his reaction to God's "love"? Do you think he was justified in his belief? How did the priest respond? *As the Christ or Holy Spirit figure, the priest responded with understanding, grace, and mercy.*

8. Read Psalm 103:13-14 above. How do you think God feels when our faith becomes messy and falters like Job's? *Like Job, we sometimes struggle and accuse Him wrongly. But God understands. He wants us to be honest with Him. Why try to hide what He already knows you are feeling? God ultimately is critical of Job's friends who defended God as though He was fragile and couldn't handle raw emotion and Job's struggle. All God wants is for us to stay engaged in life and in His love!*

CLIP #3: *He Sees Everything*

Chapter 7: ***Chateau d'If*** *(start @ 2:15 and end @ 3:30)*

---

9. What was written on the wall of his cell when Edmond arrived at Chateau d'If? *"God will give me justice."*

DORLEAC: And if you're thinking just now, "Why me, O God?" the answer is God has nothing to do with it. In fact, God is never in France this time of year.

EDMOND: God has everything to do with it. He's everywhere. He sees everything.

DORLEAC: All right, let's make a bargain, shall we? You ask God for help, and I'll stop the moment he shows up *(begins to whip Edmond).*

10. How do the words of Dorleac here mimic the Villain in our story? *The enemy wants us to believe the lie that when bad things happen, it is an indicator that we've been abandoned by God.*

11. Notice that the verse above doesn't say that God causes all things. What does it say? And how does this correspond with what God says in Psalm 94:9, Hebrews 4:13, and Romans 12:19? *It doesn't say that He causes all things, Romans 8:28 says that He causes all things (good and bad) to work for our benefit. Contrary to the villain in the story, nothing escapes God's notice, and He will act in His time when His purposes are completed. It is indeed a terrible thing to fall into the hands of a living (breathing, observant, engaged), angry God. Bottom-line: He is far better positioned to avenge than we could ever be.*

EDMOND: God has no place here priest.

ABBE FARIA: What has replaced him?

EDMOND: Revenge.

EDMOND: If you ever presume to interfere in my affairs again, I will, I promise you, finish the job I started the day we met! Do you understand?

JACOPO: I understand you are mad.

EDMOND: Mad? My enemies are falling into my traps perfectly!

JACOPO: Mad, your grace, for not seeing this: you have a fortune, a beautiful woman who loves you. Take the gold, take the woman, and live your life! Stop this plan, take what you have won!

EDMOND: I can't.

JACOPO: Why not?

EDMOND: If you ever loved me, don't rob me of my hate. It's all I have.

MERCEDES: I don't know what dark plan lies within you. Nor do I know by what design we were asked to live without each other these 16 years. But God has offered us a new beginning.

EDMOND: God?

MERCEDES: Don't slap His hand away.

12. From the quotes above, it is evident that Edmond exchanged one prison cell for another. What was that? According to Hebrews 12:15, why would God tell us that vengeance is His territory and for us to "keep out"? *He alone is qualified and able to deliver appropriate judgment. He alone can handle the responsibility. When we try, we take on bitterness, and bitterness always exacts a high price. We lose the grace of God.*
13. When Edmond got to taste the fruit of vengeance, did it heal his wounds and satisfy his soul? Explain. *No. You can especially see this at the end of the movie when he lost all taste for revenge and just wanted his family.*

CLIP #4: *Edmond the Student*
Chapter 11: ***Neglect Becomes Our Ally*** *(start @ 2:55 and end @ 12, 2:20)*

ABBE: Do not waste the light.

EDMOND: You were a soldier, priest. So you know weaponry. Teach me. Or dig alone.

ABBE: You force me to walk a fine line, Dantes . . . The stronger swordsman does not necessarily win. It is speed! Speed of hand. Speed of mind.

14. Was there grace in the midst of injustice? Did anything good come from Edmond's two captivities? If so, what? *God sent a priest who would bring healing and hope to Edmond. This priest trained him in math, Latin, logic, fencing, strategy, and ultimately gave him a map that would make him the richest man alive. His second captivity brought him friends and allies to call on when he needed their help.*
15. What does Romans 8:35-39 tell us about suffering? *Romans tells us that suffering is part of life in a fallen world—we are going to suffer. Not only is God greater than our suffering, but we cannot be separated from Him. He has promised to cause all things to work for the good. His redemption covers everything.*

Who can separate us from the love of Christ? Can affliction or anguish or persecution or famine or nakedness or danger or sword? As it is written: Because of You we are being put to death all day long; we are counted as sheep to be slaughtered. No, in all these things we are more than victorious through Him who loved us. For I am persuaded that neither death nor life, nor angels nor rulers, nor things present, nor things to come, nor powers, nor height, nor depth, nor any other created thing will have the power to separate us from the love of God that is in Christ Jesus our Lord!

ROMANS 8:35-39

CLIP #5: *God Is in Everything*
Scene 26: ***Mercedes and Edmond*** *(start @ beginning and end @ 2:30)*

MERCEDES: Why did you not come to me?

EDMOND: Why did you not wait? You married the very man who betrayed--

MERCEDES *(shows Edmond the chord around her finger)*: I told you that night on the rocks, remember? That it would never leave my finger. And it never has.

EDMOND: Why?

MERCEDES: You know why.

EDMOND: If you ever loved me, don't—don't rob me of my hate. It's all I have.

MERCEDES: Let it go, Edmond. Let it go. I don't know what dark plan lies within you. Nor do I know by what design we were asked to live without each other these sixteen years. But God has offered us a new beginning.

EDMOND: God?

MERCEDES: Don't slap His hand away.

EDMOND: Can I never escape Him?

MERCEDES: No. He is in everything.

16. What truth about God finally breaks through Edmond's pain and bitterness and sets him free? *That ultimately, God is in everything, and nothing can separate us from His love.* How can this truth be so powerful and deliver redemption to us? *It tears down strongholds that the enemy has built in our lives and reveals the truth that God is not indifferent to our lives/our pain. It is the truth of God as a relentless pursuer of our hearts that sets us free.*
17. What have you learned about God from this movie?

- *God is never the source for injustice. But he does promise never to waste it, but to use it for our benefit.*
- *God is far from indifferent. He is watching, and vengeance is His!*
- *Trust God to repay the unjust causes of pain in your life. Vengeance is His. Only He can handle it. Hatred and vengeance often destroys an individual.*
- *God wants to bring redemption into your story, and sometimes that redemption involves pain and suffering. Allow God to weave a beautiful tapestry in your life that includes faith and hope in the midst of pain and suffering.*

GOING VERTICAL

Suffering is something very real in all of our lives. We all will experience it at some point.

During this prayer time, think through the suffering that is going on.

- Be honest (Psalm 103:14)
- Trust God and each other in being able to handle raw honesty
- Thank Him in that He does not require us to take on the role of avenger. Prayerfully leave this responsibility to Him.
- Thank God that He doesn't waste our pain; that Him for redeeming what was meant to cause great harm by the enemy.

Pray that the Holy Spirit will give you the words and means to make a difference in someone else's life who is experiencing pain.

SECONDHAND LIONS

DINNER AND A MOVIE — WEEK 1

GETTING STARTED

1. Rent *Secondhand Lions*
2. Create decorating ideas
3. Review the dinner menu

SETTING THE STAGE

DÉCOR

Prior to the session, ask the person responsible for the Preschool area at church if you could borrow some of their plastic farm animals. You especially would want dogs, pigs, and chickens, but any farm animals would do. Place these on the serving table. Or, instead of farm animals, get some plastic lions and place them around the table.

DINNER

The menu items selected to accompany *Secondhand Lions* are found below. Divide the responsibility among the group members. But use your own creativity to make your movie and dinner nights special for your group. You may wish to serve corn on the cob, corn bread, homemade ice cream, or fruit cobblers with ice cream as options for this meal.

Barbequed Spare Ribs

---

1 tbsp. paprika
1 tsp. salt
1 tsp. dry mustard
1/4 tsp. chili powder
2 tbsp. Worcestershire sauce
1/4 c. vinegar
1 c. tomato juice
1/4 c. ketchup
1/2 c. water

In a saucepan, simmer ingredients for 15 minutes or until slightly thick. Put country style spare ribs or beef short ribs into casserole dish. Pour on sauce. Bake 30 minutes at 400 degrees, uncovered, and then bake at 300 degrees for 2 to 3 hours, covered.

Texas Baked Beans

1/2 pound ground beef
1 medium onion, chopped
2-16 oz. cans baked beans
1/2 cup ketchup
1 tablespoon mustard
1 tablespoon Worcestershire sauce
1 tablespoon chili powder
1/2 teaspoon salt
1/2 teaspoon pepper

Brown ground beef and onion. Drain. Mix in remaining ingredients, stirring well. Place in a 1 1/2 quart baking dish. Bake at 350 degrees for 45 minutes.

Zesty Potato Salad

4 cups cooked potatoes
1/2 cup chopped celery
2 hard cooked eggs, chopped
1/4 cup green onions, sliced
1 teaspoon salt
1/8 teaspoon pepper
1 cup mayonnaise
1 teaspoon prepared mustard
1/4 teaspoon celery seed
1 teaspoon horseradish
1 tablespoon cider vinegar

Simmer potatoes until fork tender. Remove skins, and cut into cubes. In a bowl, combine celery, eggs, potatoes, onions, vinegar, and seasonings. Toss lightly to combine. In a separate small bowl, mix mustard and salad dressing. Stir into potatoes. Refrigerate before serving.

Variation: Add cooked and crumbled bacon bits to the salad dressing and proceed as above.

Chocolate Almond Mousse

1 env. unflavored gelatin
1 1/4 c. milk
1 (6 oz.) pkg. semi-sweet chocolate pieces
1 egg
3 ice cubes
1/4 c. sugar
1/2 tsp. almond extract
1/8 tsp. salt
1 c. heavy or whipping cream
6 maraschino cherries

In a 1 quart saucepan, sprinkle gelatin evenly over 1/2 cup milk; over medium heat, warm until tiny bubbles form a round edge of saucepan and gelatin is completely dissolved, stirring frequently.

Pour hot gelatin mix into blender or food processor with knife blade attached; add chocolate pieces. Blend until chocolate is melted. Add egg, ice cubes, sugar, almond extract, salt, 1/2 cup heavy cream, and remaining 3/4 cup milk. Blend until smooth. Pour into 6 (6 ounce) freezer safe glasses. Chill in freezer 15 minutes.

Just before serving, in small bowl with mixer at high speed, beat remaining 1/2 cup heavy cream until soft peaks form. Spoon a dollop of whipping cream on top of each serving. Garnish each with a cherry.

ON THE LOOK-OUT

In almost every movie, directors and producers make a few mistakes, and those mistakes are often quite humorous. Look for these goofs in Secondhand Lions:

- At Saratoga Springs, Canada geese are shown landing. Instead of the distinctive "honk" of a goose, we hear ducks quacking.
- When the family comes to visit Hub in the hospital scene, the youngest boy is seen entering the doorway first in one shot, then in the following shot he is seen pushing past his sister to enter again.

TRIVIA ANSWERS

1. Bluebonnet
2. Pecan
3. Jalapeño
4. Sweet onion
5. Square dance

THE PROLOGUE

We recommend serving dessert after *Secondhand Lions*. Included are a few questions to begin a conversation that will continue to your next meeting.

GETTING STARTED

- Review the Bible study questions and Scripture references.
- Review the clips identified in the Bible study content. You'll want to be able to find these clips quickly and have a good handle on how they're used. Here are the Bible study clips from *Secondhand Lions* in the order they'll used during your meeting:

1. Walter Runs
   *Chapter 5: **She Lied . . . Again** (start @ beginning, end @ 2:27)*
2. *Walter Learns Not to Run*
   *Chapter 11: **Courage and Manhood** (start @ beginning, end @ 2:55)*
3. *Walter Becomes the Teacher*
   *Chapter 14: **Truth and Belief** (start @ 5:08, end @ 8:00)*
4. *Walter Finds the Courage of a Lion*
   *Chapter 17: **A Real Lion** (start @ beginning, end @ 1:25)*
5. *The Kid Gets It All*
   *Chapter 20: **Real Legends** (start @ beginning, end @ 2:55)*

Prior to the Bible study, we recommend a quick review of the movie. It will also add to the experience to show the movie trailer. Many times the theatrical trailer will be included on the DVD.

BIBLE STUDY GUIDE

REFLECTIONS

1. *What scenes from Secondhand Lions made an impact on you and why?*
2. *How did each of the characters need to find redemption in their lives? Walter? His mom? Garth? Hub?*

CLIP #1: *Walter Runs*
*Chapter 5: **She Lied . . . Again** (start @ beginning, end @ 2:27)*

GARTH: Planning your next move? Where you figure on going?

WALTER: Here. Area code 406. Montana.

GARTH: How come you're not heading to Fort Worth where your momma is?

WALTER: She's not there. She lied . . . again.

GARTH: Listen, kid, we know you got your heart set on going to Montana, but it's late. Hub, help me out here. . . . We got better maps than that one at the house, right, Hub?

HUB: Yeah, a man needs a good map, that's for sure.

WALTER: I've been to the orphan home before. I don't want to go back.

HUB: It ain't our fault you got a lousy mother.

1. Walter was in desperate need for redemption. Why? *He had been betrayed, abandoned, neglected. He was unwanted and unprotected, with no positive mother or father figure. His mother used him and put her own interests above his.* What in Walter's life needed to be redeemed? *There was a sense of abandonment that needed to be redeemed. Walter lived with a void; a loss. He needed to feel loved; he needed to feel connected to a family. He needed positive male role models who would help him to know and fulfill his potential.*
2. How would you describe the two uncles here? What were some of their obvious differences? *Hub: hurting, angry, stronger, more dominant of the two, loved danger and challenge, caring in his own way. Garth: easy-going, more sensitive, supportive, more patient, kinder, gentler, more satisfied, happy with himself.*
3. Read Isaiah 42:13 and Matthew 23:37 below. What are some of the Christlike characteristics of Hub and Garth at this point? How do each represent different aspects of God? *Hub represents the warrior aspect of God. Garth represents the tender, nurturing side—the Holy Spirit. Garth is the comforting presents that intercedes. As Hub and Garth work together Hub begins to fight for Walter. Hub fights injustice.*

CLIP #2: *Walter Learns Not to Run*
Chapter 11: ***Courage and Manhood*** *(start @ beginning, end @ 2:55)*

4. What additional characteristics of these two uncles do you learn about here? *Garth cares about his brother a great deal and wants to help. He is an encourager for his brother and wants him to find redemption and happiness. Hub feels useless, unnecessary, unneeded, less of a person, and finds it difficult to accept the losses in his life.*
5. What is it about these two men that needs redemption? How has each been drawn into the smaller stories of the enemy's schemes? How do you think Hub has bought into the lie that he is a worn out, secondhand lion? *Hub: needs to accept who he is at this stage in life; he needs to feel needed and loved. He*

needs to know that his life isn't over just because he lost Jasmine. He needs someone in whom he can invest his life. He has let himself believe the villain's lies that he is useless and life is hopeless—that he's used up. Garth, also, needs to realize that life can be more than simply sitting around and shooting at traveling salesmen. They have fallen for the villain's lies that there is little purpose in their lives, and they are comfortable with that. Both need to recapture a little "youth" and realize that there still is a great deal of life to be experienced and loved.

6. How many "secondhand lions" are in this story? What are the similarities between the real lion and the uncles? *Three. They feel caged, in a box, old and tired. They want to be free. Jasmine would like to be a "real lion" again; the uncles would like to feel like their lives still have meaning. They both need a sense of purpose, and both play a role in redeeming Walter. They all need to find a sense of connection and overcome a feeling of alienation.*

7. How do you think redemption becomes realized through Hub? Would you consider him a good role model? Why or why not? *As representative of the warrior God, redemption is realized as Hub fights for Walter and defending him against the villains in the story.*

CLIP #3: *Walter Becomes the Teacher*
Chapter 14: ***Truth and Belief*** *(start @ 5:08, end @ 8:00)*

HUB: People are basically good; that honor courage, and virtue mean everything; that power and money, money and power mean nothing; that good always triumphs over evil. And I want you to remember this, that love . . . true love never dies. You remember that, boy. You remember that. . . . A man should believe in those things because those are the things worth believing in.

WALTER: I can't be a good man until you give me the rest of the speech, right? So you need to stick around until I'm old enough to hear the whole thing. . . .

HUB: You won't be living here then.

WALTER: You're my uncle. I need you to stick around and be my uncle. What about Uncle Garth? He needs you. What about the dogs and the pig, and the lion? We all need you. I need you. . . . I know you miss Jasmine an awful, awful lot. But if you go, we'll miss you just as much. It's true.

8. Hub's life is redeemed—transformed by a 14-year-old boy. What did Hub learn about life? What did Walter give to Hub that changed him forever? How was the Villain defeated and Hub forever changed? *For the first time since Jasmine's death, Hub felt needed and loved. He felt like there was something and someone to live for. He found someone who was innocent, whose life*

needed to be redeemed from abandonment and alienation. Redemption became possible when Hub was able to let go and, as the passage says, dwell on those things that allow God to speak into his story. A 14-year-old boy gave him a new beginning in life, just as the uncles gave to Walter. When we allow God to use us as surrogates in the redemptive story of others, we are the ones who are blessed. Walter gave these two men who were isolated, miserable, and self-destructive purpose. Through Walter, God was able to work so that they could "finish well."

9. What does Walter teach us about giving to others? *An opinion question. He teaches us the importance of being connected to others, the importance of innocently loving others, the difference that one person can make in the lives of others, the power of love.*

CLIP #4: *Walter Finds the Courage of a Lion*
Chapter 17: ***A Real Lion*** *(start @ beginning, end @ 1:25)*

10. Here we meet another villain in the story. Like the larger Villain, he mixes a little truth with a great deal of lies, but ultimately is revealed for the liar he is. The villain (Stan) in *Secondhand Lions* tries to make Walter question the goodness of his uncles. How is this similar to how the Villain attacks our lives? *He tries to make us question the goodness of God's heart. He tries to cause division and destroy the connection that people need with others.*

11. In this scene, we really see two "lions." One, like our heavenly Father, was faithful and decisive when it came to protecting her "cub," giving her life for him. The other transformed "lion," Walter, saved and redeemed the lives of his two uncles. How did Walter make a difference in their lives? *Walter gave these men who were isolated, miserable, self-destructive, and angry a reason to live. He helped Garth and Hub find purpose and understand their experiences.*

12. In the beginning of the movie, Walter was a frightened, intimidated 14- year-old. Here, we see him stand up to a much bigger aggressor, and later to his mother. How can we explain the transformation in Walter's life? *Garth and Hub both taught Walter the importance of standing up for himself and what is important to him. He learned "what every man needs to know." He learned the real blessing of being connected to individuals who love him and, in turn, he can love. God is actually smitten with us. Zephaniah 3:17 tells us that He takes delight in us; that He shouts over us with shouts of joy. Matthew 23:37 suggests that He wants to gather us to Himself as a mother. God works through the surrogates Hub and Garth in Walter's life. As Walter feels their love—and warrior God's protection and delight through them—he becomes more and more indoctrinated in the masculine journey that gives him the confidence to stand-up to both the villain and the Villain.*

CLIP #5: *The Kid Gets It All*
Chapter 20: ***Real Legends*** *(start @ beginning, end @ 2:55)*

SHERIFF: Here. I found their will.

WALTER: "The kid gets it all. Just plant us in the garden with the stupid lion."

13. Just like Act IV of the Larger Story ends us for us, so, too, does Secondhand Lions end for Walter: "the kid gets it all." How is the quote below similar to 1 Corinthians 2:9? *As Christians, we need to remember that God wants to redeem all of life—even the messes. First Corinthians 2:9 reveals to us that He has prepared things for us that we cannot imagine. In the same way, Walter could never have imagined what was "prepared" for him through his surrogates, his uncles.*

GOING VERTICAL

Tonight, pray that you won't forget "Walter"—teenagers and young adults who seem lost and need redemption. If you know someone who needs a "Garth" or a "Hub," pray for the wisdom and opportunity for you to be able to give your "what every person need to know" speech about God's true Redemption.

Pray that you won't forget "Hub" or "Garth"—older folks who seem isolated and alone, who simply watch the clock, waiting for the day to hurry up and end. Is there someone you know who is waiting for "Walter" to pull up in his driveway to give is "We all need you" speech? Pray for the strength of a lion these days to make a difference in your world.

DINNER AND A MOVIE WEEK 1

DINNER AND A MOVIE

Getting Started

1. Rent *An Unfinished Life*
2. Create decorating ideas
3. Review the dinner menu

SETTING THE STAGE

DÉCOR

Tonight's theme relates to the West, but any outdoors decorations would work well. Consider boots and cowboy hats, gloves and rope, anything that would call to mind the western part of the United States. From the Internet, you could print pictures of cowboys and other TV characters from the West, such as Roy Rogers, Dale Evans, Gaby Hayes, and Trigger from *The Roy Rogers Show*; The Lone Ranger, Tonto, and Silver from *The Lone Ranger*; James Arness ("Matt Dillon"), Milburn Stone ("Doc"), Amanda Blake ("Miss Kitty") from *Gunsmoke*; Gene Barry from *Bat Masterson*; Lorne Greene and Dan Blocker from *Bonanza*; Jack Lord from *Stoney Burk*; Gene Autry from *The Gene Autry Show*; Rin Tin Tin from *The Adventures of Rin Tin Tin*; Yosemite Sam from *Bugs Bunny* cartoons; Wile E. Coyote and the Road Runner from *Looney Tunes* cartoons; Kirby Grant and Gloria Winters from *Sky King*; Robert Conrad and Ross Martin from *The Wild, Wild West*. Before the meal or the movie, you could play a matching game to see who can match the most photos with the correct TV western show or character. The person with the most matches could be the first one in line for the meal. Or, divide the group into males and females and see which group can identify the most correctly. The group with the fewest correct matches serves the winning team for the meal.

DINNER

It's always good to divide responsibilities for the meal, including clean up. Ask folks from the group to prepare an item or items for the meal and bring them. Some could simply bring paper goods and ice and soft drinks. Some could be responsible for clean up. Use these or other recipes that have a western flavor. Be certain to publicize the menu ahead of time in case some participants have special food requirements. As an added convenience, we have posted these recipes at www.SerendipityHouse.com.

Western Omelet Pie

3 tbsp. oil
1 c. onion chopped
3 1/2 c. frozen hash brown potatoes
1 1/2 tsp. salt
2 tbsp. butter
1 green pepper, chopped
2 tbsp. chopped parsley
1 1/4 c. milk
4 eggs, beaten
1 c. grated Swiss cheese

In skillet heat oil and add 1/4 cup onion; sauté until soft. Add frozen hash browns and 1 teaspoon salt. Cook over medium heat until potatoes are soft. Pat into bottom and sides of 9-inch pie plate, forming crust. Bake 20 minutes.

In the same skillet, melt butter; add pepper, remaining onions, and parsley; sauté. In medium bowl combine eggs, milk, and 1/2 teaspoon salt. Sprinkle crust with peppers, onions, and cheese. Pour in egg mixture and bake 30 minutes until set.

Fruit Salsa

1 pt. fresh strawberries, capped and diced
1 fresh ripe Anjou pear, cored and diced
1 tbsp. chopped fresh cilantro
1 tbsp. honey

Combine strawberries, pear, cilantro and honey in medium bowl. Drain and discard any liquid that has formed from the fruit.

Wyoming Whopper Cookies

2/3 c. butter
1 1/4 c. brown sugar
1 1/2 c. chunky peanut butter
2 tsp. baking soda
1 (12 oz.) pkg. chocolate chips

3 eggs, slightly beaten
3/4 c. granulated sugar
6 c. old-fashioned oats
1 1/2 c. raisins

Melt butter and blend in sugars, eggs and peanut butter; mixing well. Add oats, soda, raisins, chocolate chips. Mixture will be sticky. Drop on greased cookie sheet with an ice cream scoop or large spoon. Flatten slightly.

Bake at 350 degrees for about 15 minutes for a 3-inch cookie. Allow to cool slightly before removing to cooling rack. Makes about 2 dozen cookies.

TRIVIA ANSWERS

1. Paddington Bear
2. American Black Bear
3. Fozzie
4. Alabama
5. He didn't have a name

THE PROLOGUE

We recommend serving dessert after showing the movie. Included are a few questions to begin a conversation that will continue to your next meeting.

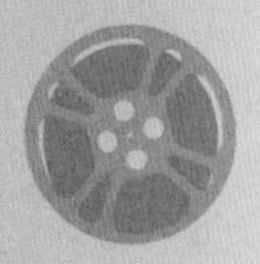

CONNECTING THE DOTS

GETTING STARTED

- Review the Bible study questions and Scripture references.
- Review the clips identified in the Bible study content. You'll want to be able to find these clips quickly and have a good handle on how they're used. Here are the Bible study clips from *An Unfinished Life* in the order they'll be used during your meeting:

1. *Jean's Confession*
   Chapter 11: ***I Killed Griffin*** *(start @ beginning and end at 3:05)*
2. *Einar's Anger Surfaces*
   Chapter 7: ***Accidents*** *(start @ beginning and end at 1:05)*
3. *The Villains*
   Chapter 1: ***We're Going to Wyoming*** *(start @ 3:38 and end at 5:35)*
4. *Mitch Deals with His Anger*
   Chapter 13: ***Mitch's Emergency*** *(start @ 3:38 and end at 5:35)*
5. *Einar and Mitch Can Relax*
   Chapter 18: ***Conclusion and Credits*** *(start @ beginning and end at 2:12)*

Prior to the Bible study we recommend a quick review of the movie. It will also add to the experience to show the movie trailer. Many times the theatrical trailer will be included on the DVD.

BIBLE STUDY GUIDE

REFLECTIONS

1. Can you remember who the characters were, the wounds they sustained, and the conflict they dealt with as a result?

   Jean . . . . A husband that was lost in a car wreck because she fell asleep at the wheel; A series of abusive relationships after that; The burden of raising a little girl on a waitress' salary

   Einar . . . . Lost his son; Lost his livelihood; Lost his wife; Lost his life; A deep resentment for Jean; Guilt because of a drunken night when he couldn't help his friend in a bear attack

   Mitch . . . . Mauled by a bear—physical and emotional scars

Griff ....Innocent eleven-year-old bystander who was dragged with her mom from bad situation to bad situation

Bear...........He was captured and held in a pen; his life as a real bear was taken from him

2. Who do you think was hurt the worst, and why?
3. Why open the movie with the bear? Notice how he is woven throughout this story. Discuss what the bear represents. *The bear represents pain. It is the wildness and unpredictability of life. The bear cannot be tamed and offers no guarantees.* How did Jesus handle the wildness and unpredictability of life (cross)? *He embraced the pain but rejected shame and guilt.*

CLIP #1: *Jean's Confession*
Chapter 11: ***I Killed Griffin*** *(begin @ 2:15)*

JEAN GILKYSON: Griffin flipped a coin and I lost. So I was the one who was driving. It was 3 o'clock in the morning and we were both tired. We wanted to make it down to the rodeo in Great Falls.

JEAN GILKYSON: I killed him, Einar. Is that what you wanna hear? It wasn't the change in our pockets, or the weak coffee, or the rain. It was me. I fell asleep and I flipped the car six times. I killed Griffin. You have no argument from me. You think it's something I forget? You think that I'm not sick with it, that I hate my life? But I tried to keep living, and you haven't. Is that why you hate me so much? You know, you act like I killed you the day Griffin died.

1. Whom did Jean refuse to forgive? *Herself.* How did Jean handle her pain? *She pursued one abusive, destructive man after another. She was unwilling to let herself love or be loved in a meaningful way.*
2. Read Hebrews 12:15. What does this verse tell us about the pitfalls of unforgiveness? *It causes trouble. It makes us sick. We think we are punishing the offender, but all we are doing is wounding ourselves.* How did unforgiveness affect Einar and Jean? *Einar lived a very bitter and lonely life because he could not forgive Jean or himself. Jean could not forgive herself and thought she should be punished for what happened that night. She thought she was only making herself pay for her actions (because she blamed herself), but her daughter also was being punished for Jean's refusal to forgive herself.*

CLIP #2: *Einar's Anger Surfaces*
Chapter 7: ***Accidents***

EINAR: Tell your kid to come down out of that tree.

JEAN: (breaks a plate) I'm sorry.

EINAR: You're sorry, huh? Well, that's just fine then.

JEAN: I'll buy you a new one.

EINAR: Oh, just that easy? Maybe I liked that plate. In fact, maybe that was my favorite . . . plate.

JEAN: It's just a plate.

EINAR: That's it, huh? Did it ever occur to you that not everything can be replaced?

3. Jean thinks it is only a plate. Discuss what this angry outburst is really about for Einar? *Pain, loss, grieving.* What does the plate remind him of? *His son's death; his own life that he feels Jean has taken from him.*
4. Not just in this scene, but throughout most of the film, why was Einar so angry? *He was angry at life, at his loss, at life's unfairness, at himself.* What was preventing him from letting go of his bitterness? *His own anger and unforgiving spirit; he wanted to be angry and let others know he was bitter.* Who were the persons he needed to forgive? *Jean, himself.*
5. In *An Unfinished Life*, what is in need of redemption? *Einar's loss and his inability to act on behalf of his friend. Mitch must again face his adversary. Jean must understand that she doesn't "deserve" the worst life has to offer.* What is standing in the way? *Standing in the way are the lies of our adversary, the devil. Einar has believed that there is nothing really worth living for after his son's death. Jean believes she is worthless—that she is the cause of suffering—her own, her daughter's, Einar's. Where Mitch is concerned—he must look danger in the eye again.*

CLIP #3: *The Villains*
Chapter 1: ***We're Going to Wyoming*** *(show 2:33-3:55)*

GARY: I don't know what happened. It's like a red mist or something comes over me and I . . . but I feel like you back me up in a corner and I . . . you do that and I hate it when I'm like that.

GRIFF: You promised—if it happened again—you promised.

6. In a broad sense, who are the villains in the movie . . .Gary? Jean? Einar? The sense of guilt/unforgiveness? The bear? The car wreck? *Gary is the obvious villain, the one who learns nothing about life. Like Jean and Einar, he blames someone else for his problems ("you back me up in a corner"), but he never understands the truth as Jean and Einar and Mitch ultimately do in the film. Einar sees Jean as a villain, responsible for his loss and pain. And Jean is trapped in the most significant ways, because she sees Gary, Einar, and even herself as villains.*
7. An unforgiving spirit was possibly the greatest villain in the story. How can unforgiveness act as a villain in our lives? *It causes bitterness. It produces a cold heart that is extremely difficult to warm again. Einar couldn't forgive Jean. Jean couldn't forgive herself. And the others—Mitch, Griff, and even the bear—were right in the middle of the pain.*

> See to it that no one falls short of the grace of God
> and that no root of bitterness springs up,
> causing trouble and by it, defiling many.
> **HEBREWS 12:15**

8. Read 1 Peter 5:8. Who is the ultimate Villain—the one trying to control each of these characters' lives—in this and every story? How do you see him at work? *Satan. Acknowledging that there is only one true villain in the story is critical to our ability to release offenses and hold the right person accountable. The truest thing about people is not their sinfulness or their offenses, but that they are first and foremost an image bearer to God. Additionally, when Christians wound us we must remember that their hearts are good (Jeremiah 31:33), but there is an enemy exploiting their stories and driving their behavior–yet they are still accountable for their decisions.* How do you see him at work? *In the life of Gary who equates manhood with abuse; in the life of Jean as she sees her life having no value, unable to forgive herself; in the life of Einar as he lives in a world of pain and unforgiveness; and indirectly in the life of Griff as she, too, is forced to deal with abuse and anger and unforgiving hearts.*

CLIP #4: *Mitch Deals with His Anger*
Chapter 13: ***Mitch's Emergency*** *(begin @ 3:38)*

EINAR: How you doin'?

MITCH: You can't just leave him there, Einar. We walked into his business. He was just doing what bears do. We can't punish him for that. Got to let him go, Einar. Get him out of that cage.

EINAR: Don't you lie here and think I could do that.

MITCH: You know I could get myself shaved in the morning, all the way dressed, too. Could probably manage to stick myself with one of those syringes if it came to it. But what I can't do is continue to lie here every day and watch you mourn for a life you think you should have had. There are people everywhere who think they got dealt a bad hand, Einar.

9. Why was Mitch so insistent here that they had to let the bear go? *It was the final step on his path to forgiveness and his own redemptive healing.* What does the bear represent? *Pain, hurt, unforgiveness.* What did the cage represent? *It was Einar himself, locked inside his own prison of unforgiveness and hate, miserable and wanting perhaps for the first time to be free.* What began finally to break in Einar's heart once he released Mitch's "bear"? *A belief that if Mitch could forgive his hurt, then perhaps Einar could forgive as well.*

10. Take note of the juxtaposition between how Einar and Jean handle their pain and need to forgive versus the way Mitch handles forgiving both the bear and Einar for being drunk. *Einar and Jean hold on to their bitterness and pain and use blame as a means to punish the "offender." Mitch wants to let go and forgive and move on with his life. Mitch embraces pain (doesn't ignore it) and rejects shame/guilt and accusations. Mitch is the Christ figure in this movie. He is modeling grace and a healthy approach to pain and life's wounds. This is a principle so many of us reverse.* Read Hebrews 12:1-2. Discuss how the principles in these verses give meaning to the characters in the movie.

11. In what ways does Mitch live life in a way similar to the model of Jesus given in Hebrews 12:2? *Mitch wants Einar to quit living his life without hope and happiness. He wants Einar to experience forgiveness. Mitch dreams and longs for the day when Einar can let go of his anger and bitterness. He is like God—who honors our free will, but His heart longs for us to know the healing and freedom (redemption) that comes when we choose forgiveness.*

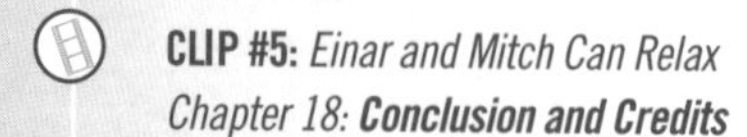

CLIP #5: *Einar and Mitch Can Relax*
Chapter 18: ***Conclusion and Credits***

EINAR: Think it might rain today.

MITCH: Naw, it's gonna stay warm.

EINAR: I didn't say anything about the temperature. I said it might rain.

MITCH: Would you bury me next to Griffin?

EINAR: Don't you think you oughtta die first?

MITCH: It's gonna happen, you know.

EINAR: Where else do you think I'd bury you? It's where my family lies. You think the dead really care about our lives?

MITCH: Yeah, I think they do. I think they forgive us our sins. I even think it's easy for them.

EINAR: Griff said you had a dream about flying.

MITCH: Yeah. I got so high, Einar. I could see where the blue turns to black. From up there, you can see all there is. And it looked like there was a reason for everything.

12. What motivation or perspective did Mitch seem to have that freed him to forgive and release his wounds? *Life is short, death is sure; there is a larger story and there is purpose for everything.*
13. What significant confession does Einar share with Jean in the hospital? *He was too drunk to help his friend Mitch when he needed Einar the most.*
14. Forgiveness brought redemption to each of these characters' lives and broke the stronghold which Satan had created. What were some of the effects of forgiveness in the lives of the characters in the movie? *Mitch—peace; Einar—brand new relationships, a new life, a new outlook on life and people, hope; Jean—a new start, a new friend and supporter, a better relationship with her daughter*
15. If forgiveness is a key weapon (2 Cor. 10), what is the relationship between "strongholds" and "redemption"? *We buy into the lies which become strongholds that require God's redemption. We are unable to overcome strongholds on our own. In* An Unfinished Life, *the inability to let go, the inability to break free from the lies—that's the stronghold that requires something greater.*
16. In 2 Corinthians 10:4-5, Paul implies we all have strongholds. What are Satan's strongholds in your life? *Anger, self-pity, unforgiveness, resentment, envy, lust, and jealousy only begin a list of possible responses to this question.*
17. How might strongholds like resentment, self-pity, envy, hostility, unhealed wounds, unforgiveness, and jealousy aid the real villain in your life? How might the Villain keep you from experiencing redemption and freedom?

Then Peter came to Him and said, "Lord, how many times could my brother sin against me and I forgive him? As many as seven times?" "I tell you, not as many as seven," Jesus said to him, "but seventy times seven."

MATTHEW 18:21-22

GOING VERTICAL

How does the Villain attack your life? We are all in need of freedom from guilt, pain, anxiety, grief, and bitterness. God has given us an incredible arsenal of ways to fight the Villain. Forgiveness is one of those weapons. As you go vertical to close tonight's meeting take these questions to God.

- God, are there areas of unforgiveness in my life? Is there an offense that needs my forgiveness? Is there an offense for which I need to be forgiven?
- How is my unforgiveness keeping me captive?

Take these questions to your heart.

- Am I willing to utilize the awesome spiritual weapon of forgiveness against the real Villain?
- If not, then why do I yield? If yes, then how will I deploy it?

SEABISCUIT

DINNER AND A MOVIE — WEEK 1

GETTING STARTED

1. Rent *Seabiscuit*
2. Create decorating ideas
3. Review the dinner menu

SETTING THE STAGE

DÉCOR

Decorations for this event can be simple. You will need a few helium balloons, a few sheets of thick construction paper (one for each small group), a plastic toy horse, a small table, felt-tip markers, and a name tag for each participant. Create a "Winner's Circle" using a few helium-filled balloons. (This can be as simple as placing a group of three balloons on both ends of a small table.) If possible, borrow a plastic toy horse from the children's area of your church. Before dinner, divide the larger group into smaller groups of four. Give each group a small piece of cardboard or thick construction paper folded in half for a name placard. Give each person a name tag. The group should decide who will be the jockey, owner, trainer, and "stable-master" (the one who cleans out the stables). They should write their job title on their name tag. Ask each group to name their horse and be able to share why they chose that name. They should write the horse's name on the placard. Each group gets a turn to stand in the winner's circle with the horse; place the placard where everyone can see their horse's name, and share why they gave their horse that name. Take several photos of each group in the winner's circle and send them via e-mail to all of the participants between the two meetings. You also could print them and display the photos for the next session.

DINNER

The four menu items for this dinner and a movie night fit perfectly with a movie about a race horse. If members of the group are bringing items, remember to give participants as much advance notice as possible. Because the ham will be the most expensive item, you may want to ask participants (or couples) to bring $1.00 or $2.00 to help reimburse the person bringing that item. The recipes have been posted at www.SerendipityHouse.com for your convenience.

Spiced Mustard-Glazed Ham

1 fully cooked ham, boneless, about 5 pounds
1 jar (16 to 18 ounces) orange marmalade
1 tablespoon plus 2 teaspoons dry mustard
1/2 cup spicy brown mustard
1 clove garlic, minced
1/2 teaspoon ground ginger

Place ham on a rack in roasting pan, fat side up. Score fat of ham in a diamond pattern. Combine remaining ingredients, stirring until well blended. Refrigerate half of the mixture. Brush ham with remaining half of mixture.

Bake ham at 350° for about 2 hours, or until a meat thermometer registers 140° F. Brush with the remaining marmalade mixture every 15 to 20 minutes. .

Green Beans with Lemon

1/2 pound green beans
1 teaspoon fresh lemon juice
1 teaspoon finely chopped fresh flat-leafed parsley leaves (wash and dry before chopping)
1/2 teaspoon freshly grated lemon zest
Freshly ground black pepper to taste

Trim regular green beans and cook in a large saucepan of boiling salted water until crisp and tender (approximately 3 to 4 minutes). Drain in a colander. In a bowl toss beans with lemon juice, parsley, lemon zest, and pepper, and season with salt.

Corn Pudding

3 eggs, slightly beaten
2 cups whole kernel corn, cooked and drained
2 cups milk, scalded
1/3 cup finely chopped onion
1 tablespoon butter, melted
1 teaspoon sugar
1 teaspoon salt

Combine ingredients; pour into greased 1 1/2 quart casserole. Set in shallow pan; fill pan with one inch of hot water. Bake at 350 degrees for 40-45 minutes or till knife inserted in center comes out clean. Then let stand 10 minutes at room temperature so that center can firm up.

Derby Pie

1 cup sugar
2 eggs
1/3 cup self-rising flour
1 teaspoon vanilla
1/2 cup chocolate chips
1 cup pecans
1 stick margarine, melted

Mix all ingredients and bake in an unbaked pie shell for 40-45 minutes at 350 degrees.

ON THE LOOK-OUT

In almost every movie, directors and producers make a few mistakes, and those mistakes are often quite humorous. Look for these goofs in Seabiscuit:

- Look at the montage of still photographs purporting to show the first year of the Great Depression.
- In the montage, a truck is visible with a 1937 license plate.
- During Seabiscuit's Santa Anita Handicap win, he is shown to be running dead last early in the race. But this isn't correct.
- The charts for the real 1940 Santa Anita Handicap show Seabiscuit to be no worse than fourth at any point during the race, and in fact he was in perfect striking position around the first turn and down the backstretch.

TRIVIA ANSWERS

1. Buick
2. 2
3. Man o' War
4. Pimlico

THE PROLOGUE

We recommend serving dessert after watching *Seabiscuit*. Included are a few questions to begin a conversation that will continue to your next meeting.

GETTING STARTED

- Review the Bible study questions and Scripture references.
- Review the clips identified in the Bible study content. You'll want to be able to find these clips quickly and have a good handle on how they're used. (NOTE: This movie has no chapter titles. In addition, the viewing times run concurrently; they do not begin at 00 for each chapter.)

  Here are the Bible study clips from Seabiscuit in the order they'll be used during your meeting:

1. *Seabiscuit's History*
   Chapter 9: (Start @ 46:00 and end @ 47:05)
2. *You Don't Throw a Whole Life Away*
   Chapter 8: (Start @ beginning and end @ 42:00)
3. *He Can Do Great Things*
   Chapter 14: (Start @ 1:07:55 and end @ 1:08:48)
4. *He Fixed Us*
   Chapter 25: (Start @ 2:11:00 and end @ 2:12:10)

Prior to the Bible study, we recommend a quick review of the movie. It will also add to the experience to show the movie trailer. Many times the theatrical trailer will be included on the DVD.

BIBLE STUDY GUIDE

REFLECTIONS

1. Which scenes in Seabiscuit impacted you the most? Why?
2. What single thread wove itself through all of the characters' lives? *Pain and loss.*
3. In *Seabiscuit* we find a group of people (and an animal) coming together to achieve a specific goal. Who were they? How were they alike? What was their bond? *Seabiscuit—A horse with a tough upbringing, too small, not easily handled or trained, a loser in racing circles; Red Pollard—the jockey—A kid with a tough upbringing, he found himself fighting on the side to make ends meet; Charles Howard—the car dealer—Made his fortune, but had a tough blow to his life when he lost his son in a car accident, then lost his wife in divorce; Tom Smith—the trainer—A vagabond with a tough life, not much security, passed over too many times.*

4. How was each character wounded? *Red: Abandoned and betrayed by those who were supposed to watch out for him; Tom: He was of no use. His existence didn't matter; Charles: Loss of a child, a dream, and ultimately his marriage.* How was each of these characters wounded? What different ways did each character deal with or live out his wounds? *Tom: Isolation; Red: Isolation, unhealthy independence, fighting and destructive behavior, and a general tone of anger towards people; Charles: Used entertainment and partying to numb the pain; Seabiscuit: Rage, wanted to be left alone.*

5. What does Isaiah 61:1-2 imply that we all need? *We are all in bondage that needs to be broken. We all have wounds that need to be healed. We all have broken hearts that need to be bound. We all have glory that awaits restoration.*

CLIP #1: *Seabiscuit's History*
Chapter 9: (Start @ 46:00 and end @ 47:05)

NARRATOR: The first time he saw Seabiscuit, the colt was walking through the fog at 5:00 in the morning. Smith would say later that the horse looked right through him, as if to say, "What are you looking at? Who do you think you are?" . . . They made him a training partner to better horses, forcing him to lose head-to-head duels to boost the confidence of the other animal. Soon he grew as bitter and angry as his sire Hard Tack had been. He was sold for the rock bottom price of $2,000. And, of course, it all made sense. . . . When they finally did race him, he did just what they had trained him to do. He lost.

1. How do the characters' similarities in this movie mirror what we oftentimes see today in people's lives? *If people lose enough times, eventually they become hopeless, bitter, and angry unless there is a loving community to help; Broken lives all around us; We need someone to believe in us; We have to earn our victories; There are very few "born-winners." Most of us come from the rear; We can see it in ourselves, too. We don't like to admit it, but the bitterness and anger towards life—sometimes it's there.*

2. How does Seabiscuit's story actually parallel Red's story? *Like Red, he was neglected, abused, abandoned, wounded, angry. Soon after Red hurt his leg, Seabiscuit hurt his leg. There was a bond of empathy between this horse and Red that was vital to Red's redemption.*

CLIP #2: *You Don't Throw a Whole Life Away*
Chapter 8: (Start @ beginning and end @ 42:00)

CHARLES: Who's that?

MAN: Huh? Oh, he's a crackpot. Lives alone in the bushes.

CHARLES: What's he do?

MAN: I don't know. He used to be a trainer, farrier. Now he just looks after that horse. Come on. Let's look at another barn.

(later)

TOM: Howdy.

CHARLES: Hello. (referring to a horse) Will he get better?

TOM: Already is . . . a little.

CHARLES: Will he race?

TOM: No. Not that one.

CHARLES: So why are you fixing him?

TOM: 'Cause I can. Every horse is good for somethin'. He could be a cart horse or a lead pony. And he's still nice to look at. You know, you don't throw a whole life away just 'cause he's banged up a little.

3. Wounds can be handled in many ways. Read Jeremiah 6:14. What does this verse say about the way we sometimes handle the wounds of others? Why is God so critical of us in Jeremiah 6:14? *Here, God was critical of the prophets and priests for dealing with people's wounds superficially. The church sometimes does this when there is a superficial focus on having faith and prayer, in other words, a "band-aid" approach to healing. We offer prayer and words of comfort, but we do nothing to help the actual cause of the wounds. The need for a sense of deep healing is not achieved, and there is no hope shared. We need to focus less on the symptoms in the lives of others and start focusing on the true cause. A redemptive community helps people process their wounds and provides a safe place to deal with shameful, painful parts of our stories.*

CLIP #3: *He Can Do Great Things*
Chapter 14: (Start @ 1:07:55 and end @ 1:08:48)

NARRATOR: In the end, it wasn't the dams or the roads or the bridges or the parks. Or the tunnels or the thousands of other public projects that were built in those years. It was more invisible than that. Men who were broken only a year before suddenly felt restored. Men who'd been shattered suddenly found their voice.

CHARLES: Well, I just think this horse has a lot of heart. He may have been down, but he wasn't out. He may have lost a few, but he didn't let it get to him. We could all learn a lick or two from this little guy. Oh, and by the way, he doesn't know he's little. He thinks he's the biggest horse out there. . . . See, sometimes when the little guy, he doesn't know he's a little guy, he can do great big things.

4. As the movie progressed, what became the characters' bond (beyond their brokenness)? How did they experience redemption? *In the beginning of their relationship, their bond was a sense of hopelessness, yet these people found something within themselves and in each other that brought them out of their old behavior. They started to win; They started to gain confidence again; They started to trust each other; They found new energy and purpose; They found a sense of personal redemption in a community of individuals who cared for each other and would not give up on each other.*

5. In the Christian community, how successful do you think the church is at helping people achieve this kind of personal redemption? Why? Can you share a brief example?

6. How was their connection—their bond of community—important to each other's success? *Something about their connection made them better. The team created a cycle of validation, affirmation, redemption, confidence, and love. They never could have accomplished what they achieved apart from each other.*

7. Read Mark 3:13-14. What was the first reason given for Jesus' calling of The Twelve? Talk a little about the "be-with" factor. *In a loving community (that is, free of isolation) we cannot escape who we really are. In isolation we can fool ourselves; we can make ourselves believe lies told by the Villain. In community and over time, we are encouraged to look deep inside of ourselves for the truth and deal with what we see. In community we find accountability, warning, evaluation—and—encouragement, love, empathy. Jesus' redemptive mission includes salvation, healing, setting captives free, and restoration. All of these elements should be present in a redemptive community. Redemptive community encompasses much more than relationships.*

CLIP #4: *He Fixed Us*

Chapter 25: (Start @ 2:11:00 and end @ 2:12:10)

8. Why do you suppose in James 5:16 God encourages us to tell our stories to one another and even reveal our sins (secrets)? *God knows that isolation—being alone with our secrets—can make us sick, angry, and even more isolated. One of the primary weapons in the enemy's toolbox is to isolate us and make us feel that God doesn't care about our loneliness and struggle. True redemptive community is vital for life. Everyone needs it; no one can or should try to face the issues of life alone. Could it be that wounded people are drawn to wounded people? Could it be that there something substantial about those who have survived trauma?*

9. Read Proverbs 20:5. How does the principle of asking clarifying questions and seeking to be discerning in one another's lives apply to the healing process? How is it demonstrated in this movie? *It is important to have people in our lives who know how to ask perceptive, provocative, and sometimes demanding (but never critical) questions. We need people who care about us and are willing to ask about our lives and our needs. Remember Marcela's questions:*

   "So do you feel better? No? How could you?" and Charles' question to Red: "Son, What are you so angry about?"

10. Read 1 Peter 4:8. From the movie, can you remember scenes where empathy (deep love) played a critical role in each of these folk's redemptive journey? How do these scenes help us to understand the 1 Peter passage? *Charles Howard having coffee and seeking out Tom in the night (dark night of his soul); Giving Red the money for dental work and encouraging him to eat; Reminding Tom of his own words that no one is disposable; The care that Charles showed Red when he was hurt; The empathy Marsela demonstrated to Charles in Mexico when they first met, and when Charles was struggling over letting Red go; George was so compassionate and loving to Red, even when Red resented him for it. We can make mistakes in trying to care for one another, but true care and love can overcome mistakes and make us stronger as individuals and as a community.*

11. Typically when we are moved by a story, it is because it is either borrowing from the larger story of life, from our own story, or both. Which is it for you? What part of this movie made you stop and think? Why do you think this is the case? *Spend a good amount of time here. Let the stories flow with a lot of encouragement and affirmation of those who share. This could be the most powerful part of your study this week*

GOING VERTICAL

Tom says, "You don't throw a whole life away just 'cause he's banged up a little." *Seabiscuit* implies rather openly that we're all banged up a little, yet all worth saving. In fact, our wounds can make us beautiful in the light of God's redemptive story. Jesus says that He came to give us a crown of beauty instead of ashes (Is. 61:3; Luke 4:18-19). This Connecting the Dots experience reveals the power of community as God fulfills His promise of ultimate redemption. As you close this study of redemption pray in the following way.

- Help us live and experience real redemptive community.
- God, we want and need more of You. Just like all of the characters in the story, we're banged up.
- Give us courage to tell our stories–our true stories. Give us the strength to share our messes so you can work through our community.
- Instill in us a passion that accepts nothing less than true redemptive community.

NOTES

WELCOME TO COMMUNITY

WELCOME TO COMMUNITY!

Meeting together with a group of people to study God's Word and experience life together is an exciting adventure. A small group is . . . a group of people unwilling to settle for anything less than redemptive community.

CORE VALUES

COMMUNITY

God is relational, so He created us to live in relationship with Him and each other. Authentic community involves sharing life together and connecting on many levels with the people in our group.

GROUP PROCESS

Developing authentic community requires a step-by-step process. It's a journey of sharing our stories with each other and learning together.

STAGES OF DEVELOPMENT

Every healthy group goes through various stages as it matures over a period of months or years. We begin with the birth of a new group, deepen our relationships in the growth and development stages, and ultimately multiply to form other new groups.

INTERACTIVE BIBLE STUDY

God provided the Bible as an instruction manual of life. We need to deepen our understanding of God's Word. People learn and remember more as they wrestle with truth and learn from others. The process of Bible discovery and group interaction will enhance our growth.

EXPERIENTIAL GROWTH

The goal of studying the Bible together is not merely a quest for knowledge; this should result in real life change. Beyond solely reading, studying, and dissecting the Bible, being a disciple of Christ involves reunifying knowledge with experience. We do this by bringing our questions to God, opening a dialogue with our hearts (instead of killing our desires), and utilizing other ways to listen to God speak to us (group interaction, nature, art, movies, circumstances, etc.). Experiential growth is always grounded in the Bible as God's primary means of revelation and our ultimate truth-source.

THE POWER OF GOD

Our processes and strategies will be ineffective unless we invite and embrace the presence and power of God. In order to experience community and growth, Jesus needs to be the centerpiece of our group experiences and the Holy Spirit must be at work.

REDEMPTIVE COMMUNITY

Healing best happens within the context of community and in relationship. A key aspect of our spiritual development is seeing ourselves through the eyes of others, sharing our stories, and ultimately being set free from the secrets and the lies we embrace that enslave our souls.

MISSION

God has invited us into a larger story with a great mission. It is a mission that involves setting captives free and healing the broken-hearted (Isaiah 61:1-2). However, we can only join in this mission to the degree that we've let Jesus bind up our wounds and set us free. As a group experiences true redemptive community, other people will be attracted to that group, and through that group to Jesus. We should be alert to inviting others while we maintain (and continue to fill) an "empty chair" in our meetings to remind us of others who need to encounter God and authentic Christian community.

SHARING YOUR STORIES

The sessions in *Finding Redemption in the Movies* are designed to help you share a little of your personal lives with the other people in your group. Through your time together, each member of the group is encouraged to move from low risk, less personal sharing to higher risk communication. Real community will not develop apart from increasing intimacy of the group over time.

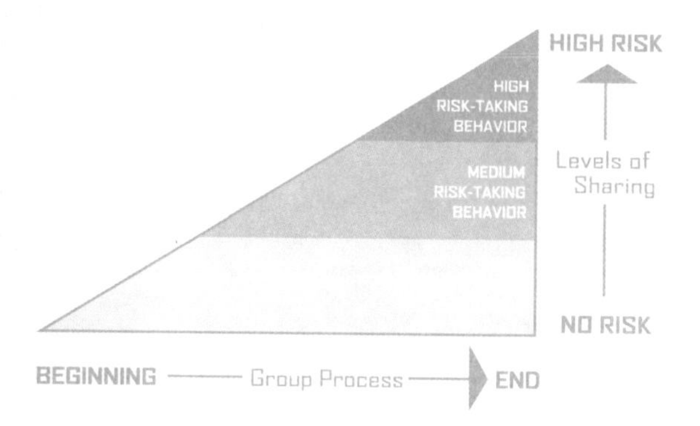

SHARING YOUR LIVES

As you share your lives together during this time, it is important to recognize that it is God who has brought each person to this group, gifting the individuals to play a vital role in the group (1 Corinthians 12:1). Each of you has been uniquely designed to contribute in your own unique way to building into the lives of the other people in your group. As you get to know one another better, consider the following four areas that will be unique for each person. These areas will help you get a "grip" on how you can better support others and how they can support you.

G – **Spiritual Gifts**: God has given you unique spiritual gifts (1 Corinthians 12; Romans 12:3-8; Ephesians 4:1-16; etc.).

R – **Resources**: You have resources that perhaps only you can share, including skill, abilities, possessions, money, and time (Acts 2:44-47; Ecclesiastes 4:9-12, etc.).

I – **Individual Experiences**: You have past experiences, both good and bad, that God can use to strengthen others (2 Corinthians 1:3-7; Romans 8:28, etc.).

P – **Passions**: There are things that excite and motivate you. God has given you those desires and passions to use for His purposes (Psalm 37:4,23; Proverbs 3:5-6,13-18; etc.).

To better understand how a group should function and develop in these four areas, consider going through the Serendipity study entitled *Great Beginnings*.

LEADING A SMALL GROUP

LEADING A SMALL GROUP

You will find a great deal of helpful information in this section that will be crucial for success as you lead your group.

Reading through this and utilizing the suggested principles and practices will greatly enhance the group experience. You need to accept the limitations of leadership. You cannot transform a life. You must lead your group to the Bible, the Holy Spirit, and the power of Christian community. By doing so your group will have all the tools necessary to draw closer to God and each other, and to experiencing heart transformation.

Make the following things available at each session:

- *Finding Redemption in the Movies* book for each attendee
- Bible for each attendee
- Snacks and refreshments
- Pens or pencils for each attendee

THE SETTING AND GENERAL TIPS

1. Prepare for each meeting by reviewing the material, praying for each group member, asking the Holy Spirit to join you, and making Jesus the centerpiece of every experience.
2. Create the right environment. Set the room temperature at 69 degrees and make sure pets are in a location where they cannot interrupt the meeting. Have music playing as people arrive (volume low enough for people to converse) and, if possible, burn a sweet-smelling candle.
3. Have soft drinks and coffee available for Connecting the Dots early arrivals.
4. Have someone with the spiritual gift of hospitality ready to make any new attendees feel welcome.
5. Be sure there is adequate lighting so that everyone can read without straining.
6. There are four types of questions used in each session: Observation (What is the passage telling us?), Interpretation (What does the passage mean?), Self-revelation (How am I doing in light of the truth unveiled?), and Application (Now that I know what I know, what will I do to integrate this truth into my life?). You won't be able to use all the questions in each study, but be sure to use some from each.

7. Connect with group members away from group time. The amount of participation you have during your group meetings is directly related to the amount of time you connect with your group members away from the meeting time.
8. Don't get impatient about the depth of relationship group members are experiencing. Building real Christian community takes time.
9. Be sure pens and/or pencils are available for attendees at each meeting.
10. Never ask someone to pray aloud without first getting their permission.

LEADING MEETINGS

1. The meeting should feel like a conversation from beginning to end, not a classroom experience.
2. Be certain every member responds to the Prologue and Reflection questions. The goal is for every person to hear his or her own voice early in the meeting. People will then feel comfortable to converse later on. If members can't think of a response, let them know you'll come back to them after the others have spoken.
3. Remember, a great group leader talks less than 10% of the time. If you ask a question and no one answers, just wait. If you create an environment where you fill the gaps of silence, the group will quickly learn they needn't join you in the conversation.
4. Don't be hesitant to call people by name as you ask them to respond to questions or to give their opinions. Be sensitive, but engage everyone in the conversation.
5. Don't ask people to read aloud unless you have gotten their permission prior to the meeting. Feel free to ask for volunteers to read.
6. Watch your time. If discussion time is extending past the time limits suggested, offer to the option of pressing on into other discussions or continuing the current session into your next meeting. REMEMBER: People and their needs are always more important than completing all the questions.

THE GROUP

Each small group has its own persona. Every group is made up of a unique set of personalities, backgrounds, and life experiences. This diversity creates a dynamic distinctive to that specific group of people. Embracing the unique character of your group and the individuals in that group is vital to group members experiencing all you're hoping for.

Treat each person as special, responsible, and valuable members of this Christian community. By doing so you'll bring out the best in each of them, thus creating a living, breathing, life-changing group dynamic.

YOU CAN HELP GROUP MEMBERS THROUGH …

Support

Provide plenty of time for support among the group members. Encourage members to connect with each other between meetings as they can.

Shared Feelings

Reassure the members that their feelings are very normal in a situation such as they are in. Encourage the members to share their feelings with one another.

Advice Giving

Avoid giving advice. Encourage cross-talk (members talking to each other), but limit advice giving. "Should" and "ought" to statements tend to increase the guilt the loss has already created.

Silence

Silence is not a problem. Even though it may seem awkward, silence is just a sign that people are not ready to talk. It DOES NOT mean they aren't thinking or feeling. If the silence needs to be broken, be sure you break it with the desire to move forward.

Prayer

Prayer is vital to personal and community growth. Starting and ending with prayer is important. However, people may need prayer in the middle of the session. Here's a way to know when the time is right to pray. If a member is sharing and you sense a need to pray, then begin to look for a place to add it.

NOTES

other great small-group

GOD & THE ARTS

Where faith intersects life.

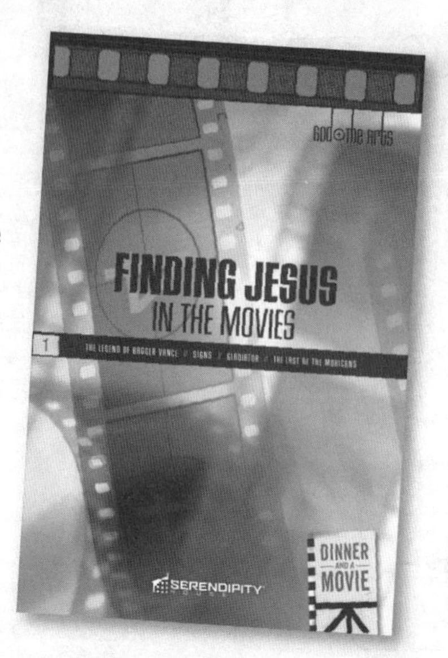

The *God and the Arts* series continues with *Finding Jesus in the Movies,* another great Dinner and a Movie small-group experience. This study reveals how the great stories only re-tell the greatest story—the story of the gospel—written in the heart of us all. Movies to view include *Gladiator, Signs,* and *The Legend of Bagger Vance.* Your small group will discover through story a deeper understanding of redemption and how God is making all things new in your life.

Finding Jesus in the Movies
1574943553

FOUNDATIONS

Experience the mystery for the first time. Again.

Jesus seemed to love paradox and often taught by asking questions rather than dumping information. It's an idea we can all connect with—an idea we all struggle with. At some point in our lives, we've had questions—"Who is God" and "Where was He when...". God can handle these questions and desires the intimacy that comes from working through them. *The Foundations of the Faith* series takes groups through this process.

Foundational Truths
1574943111

Knowing Jesus
1574943103

The Christian in a Postmodern World
1574941089

God and the Journey to Truth
1574941097

ACKNOWLEDGMENTS

We pray that God will work through these stories to reveal the crucial role you have been called and created to fill in the Larger Story—an epic more real than the physical world we inhabit. Serendipity House would like to acknowledge Kevin Colon and Richard Ryan for the work they put into the manuscript. We also acknowledge the following for their roles in completing *Finding Redemption in the Movies.*

Writer
Ron Keck

Editorial Team
Brian Daniel
Richard Ryan
Stacey Owens
Sarah Hogg

Cover + Interior Design
Brian Marschall